The Embroidered Countryside

The Embroidered Countryside

RICHARD BOX

B.T. BATSFORD LTD, LONDON

For my Mother with love

Unless otherwise stated, all illustrations and photographs are by the author.

ACKNOWLEDGEMENTS

I am indebted to many people for their part in the production of this book. I now take this happy opportunity to give them my thanks for all their encouragement and help.

To Daphne Ashby, Helena Baily, Miranda Brookes, Julia Caprara, Josie Durham, Margaret Flintham, Margaret Hall-Townley, Doreen Hooper, Ashton James, Heide Jenkins, Maureen King, Rita Marsland, Jean Muchelec, Brian Nevitt, Eirian Short, Pauline Thomas, Audrey Walker and Verina Warren.

To Rosalind Dace, my editor, for her enthusiastic encouragement, long-suffering forbearance and kind reassurances.

To Pauline Garnham for her time, energy and patience in typing the manuscript so cheerfully.

Finally, to all of you who have liked looking at my embroideries and paintings, enjoyed attending my talks and courses, and who continually encourage me in all my endeavours.

First published 1994

© Richard Box 1994

Typeset by Goodfellow & Egan, Cambridge
and printed in Singapore

Published by
B.T. Batsford Ltd
4 Fitzhardinge Street
London W1H 0AH

British Library Cataloguing-in-Publication Data
A catalogue record for this book is available from the British Library.

ISBN 0 7134 7272 3

Contents

INTRODUCTION

Sunrise

I am gone into the fields
To take what this sweet hour yields.

Percy Bysshe Shelley

Dear Reader,

Welcome to our journey through the country-side! The continuous pageant of seasons shows its multifarious changes and subtle variations on fields and woodlands, hills and valleys, rivers and meadows and on all the creatures that dwell therein. It comes as no surprise that this source of natural beauty is beloved of painters and poets alike. Embroiderers also have found much inspiration from such wonders.

Therefore all seasons shall be sweet to thee,
Whether the summer clothe the general earth
With greenness, or the redbreast sit and sing
Betwixt the tufts of snow on the bare branch
Of mossy apple-tree

Samuel Taylor Coleridge, *Frost At Midnight*

This book is written for those of you who wish to maintain this tradition. For many years I have been drawing, painting and embroidering different aspects of the countryside, with particular emphasis on flowers. I am delighted to be able to extend my repertoire to include fauna as well as flora in this book.

Now the bright morning star, day's harbinger,
Comes dancing from the east, and leads with her
The flowery May, who from her green lap throws
The yellow cowslip and the pale primrose.

John Milton, *Song on May Morning*

My wish is to develop some of the ideas I introduced in my first book, *Drawing and Design for Embroidery: a course for the fearful* (Batsford); the last chapter is expanded in my second and most recent book, *Flowers for Embroidery* (David and Charles).

Some of you may be experienced embroiderers, some of you may be nervous beginners. Be assured that it really does not matter what you consider your ability to be, or not to be! Far more important is that you are willing to have a go, and to try the projects in this book. You shall all be treated the same, as if we have never met before. In this sense, I shall consider you all as beginners because you are all embarking on this particular journey for the first time.

I suggest you use this book logically and sequentially. The first project, a cluster of primroses, lays the foundations for all the other projects. The procedures, methods and techniques of the subsequent projects vary, but each is dependent in terms of your understanding of the ones preceding it. Therefore, exercise discipline! Read each chapter in turn and engage in each project as it is presented. You will make your path more accessible in this journey, your way will be clearer and your travelling will become more enjoyable.

This leads to my final suggestion, which is that you try to approach each project in a relaxed, but alert, state of mind. We have all experienced that if we engage in an activity in a state of unrest or agitation, we usually make mistakes. If we approach our projects in a state of quiet and peaceful attention, our tasks are more likely to proceed smoothly and efficiently. Most important of all, they will be much more enjoyable to do. If you know any simple relaxation exercises to help your mind and body to become calm and free of impeding agitations, then please try and remember to practise them. Let us try one such exercise now.

1. Sunrise, 1993. Free machine embroidery in
granite stitch.

Sit in an upright chair with both feet on the ground. Allow your body to sag and your limbs to go floppy. Close your eyes and take a slightly longer time to breathe in and out. Now slowly straighten up your body. Allow it to become erect and alert, without being rigid or tense. Place your hands in your lap. Ensure that your head is upright and in alignment with your body, but keep your eyes gently closed. Focus your mind on the sense of touch to begin with. Notice your feet touching the ground, and how they are touched by their coverings, whether these be socks, stockings or tights, and how these are surrounded by your shoes. Notice how other clothing touches the different parts of your body. Also notice how the air touches the bare parts of your body. Become aware of its temperature. If you allow your jaw to drop as it relaxes, you will notice the touch of air on the upper and lower lips, the tongue, the gums, the palate and the back of the throat. Now shift the attention from the sense of touch to the sense of listening. Listen to the sound of your breathing to start with. Listen to the drawing in of the breath through the nose and your letting it go out through the mouth. If you focus on this sound very carefully you will notice very slight changes in both pitch and volume within the sounds you hear. In this way, listen to the sounds that are presented to you from the room in which you are sitting. Then listen to the sounds beyond the room, within the building and also outside the building. Listen to each sound as it comes and let it go as it goes. You will discover an amazing range of sounds hitherto dismissed as ordinary and uninteresting. This is because they had not been given your interest. *That which is given interest becomes interesting.*

Next, open your eyes and allow them to rest on the first object they choose for you. Do not attend to an idea you might put in your mind that the object is boring. Boredom is an attitude residing in the mind, not in objects! Simply allow your eyes to rest on this object and look at it in the following way. First, allow your eyes to follow the outer edges of its contours. Notice whether these edges are straight or curved, or a combination of both. If you see straight edges, notice at what angles they lie. Are some towards a vertical, more towards a horizontal or more obviously diagonal? If you see curved edges, notice the various directions of these contours and whether they are open or more closed curves. Now look within the object and observe the range of light and dark passages. This range is known as either 'value', 'tonal value' or just 'tone'. The object you have chosen may have light and dark passages as intrinsic parts of its make-up, such as printing or patterning. Thus you will see some variation of tone because of this. However, light on the object causes highlights and casts shadows. Hence, there are two causes for a variety of tonal values which are there to be seen. Lastly, look at the colour of the object. If it is multicoloured, choose one of its most salient colours. If it seems not to be any particular colour (grey, brown, white or black), do not be perturbed! Very soon we shall learn to accept everything as coloured. In order to assess the colour of this object, it is helpful to select another object nearby (or part of another object) of the same colour category. Then cast your eyes from one to the other to see if you are able to detect a slight difference of hue between these two similar colours. For example, the colour of your first chosen object may be green; by comparing it with your second chosen object, it appears a definite blue-green compared to the yellow-green of the other object. Another example, which may take a little practice to see, is the variety of colour hues within the colour known as black. John Ruskin said of Velasquez, 'There is more colour in his black than most painters have in their palettes!'

If you have never engaged in this kind of relaxed attention exercise before, try it for a few minutes to begin with, then progress to 5 and even 10 minutes as your daily practice increases and develops in concentration. At first, you may find your mind wanders. Do not worry unduly about this and avoid reprimanding it at all costs. When you notice that it has gone away on its own little 'trip' somewhere, simply and gently direct it back on course again. The mind is always active; it is always attending to something. In order to help it to become attentively calm and calmly attentive, it needs gentle discipline such as this. In medical circles, such exercises are practised more and more, and are becoming accepted as genuine methods to aid healing, particularly the relief of stress. In religious circles, this discipline is as old as the religions themselves. In the West it is known as contemplation, in the East it is known as meditation.

Those of you who have encountered my methods before, will know this attentive exercise as the 'Golden Cord'. You will remember that the body becomes relaxed and alert simultaneously if we imagine a glittering golden cord, which comes from Heaven, attached to the top of the head. The piano teacher who gave me this analogy was taught it by her teacher and found it a very useful way to maintain her proper posture.

If you follow these suggestions before and during the projects throughout this book, you should find that your practice will flow easily and fluently.

CHAPTER ONE

Spring

Nothing is so beautiful as Spring —
When weeds, in wheels, shoot long and lovely
*   and lush;*
Thrush's eggs look little low heavens, and thrush
Through the echoing timber does so rinse and
*   wring*
The ear, it strikes like lightnings to hear him
*   sing*

Gerard Manley Hopkins, *Spring*

Spring is the season when many of us redis-
cover the delight of the natural world after the
long and wearisome winter months. It is
depicted in art and literature as the season
when life renews itself, and it is often portrayed
as the season of love. It is when the earth casts
off its icy mantle of frost and snow, and the air
is brisk with boisterous breezes. Lambs gambol
in the fields, hibernating creatures come out to
play, the first swallow is seen and the first
cuckoo is heard. Blossom buds burst out to greet
us and the mossy banks offer their gifts of snowdrops, violets, celandines and primroses. All is
sweet and lovely, in perfect order and with sur-
prising harmonies. Although each season pos-
sesses its own particular treasures, there is a
special delight in our hearts at the very first
glimpse of spring.

2. Bluebell Wood, 1993. Fabric collage with
machine and hand embroidery. Photograph by
Ashton James.

Primroses

Dost ask me, why I send thee here,
This firstling of the infant year —
This lovely native of the vale,
That hangs so pensive and so pale?

Robert Burns, *The Primrose*

THE INSPIRATION

The delicately coloured primrose is one of the best-loved and the prettiest of our native wild-flowers. Its arrival is eagerly awaited because it is one of the early signs of spring. Its name is derived from the Latin *primrosa*, the first rose. It blooms in great abundance during March and April, when the simple symmetry of its five-petalled flowers attracts the eye and gladdens the heart. During my four years in Herefordshire, where I now live, the primroses in my garden have multiplied many times, and every year I give myself a treat by ensuring that I make a number of studies in paint and pencil. I have chosen a drawing I made with coloured pencils to act as the inspiration and guide for our first project. This will include fabric collage and some simple machine and hand embroidery techniques.

USING THE SOURCES OF INSPIRATION

If you prefer to use another picture of primroses, by all means do so. There is a treasure store of information close to you; your local library will have a section on natural history, with many illustrated books. Calendars, posters and greetings cards provide plenty of source material, and seed catalogues from your nearest garden centre will also give you a rich supply of visual data.

Some of you may be concerned about the laws of copyright. If someone's work is reproduced exactly, permission from the author or artist must be sought. However, if it is used as a starting point for the kind of free translation in

fabric collage, machine and hand embroidery we shall be doing in this book, no such permission is needed. Nevertheless, if you hold an exhibition of your work for personal gain, it is deemed courteous to acknowledge the source of its origin.

Some of you who are proficient might like to use one of your own paintings or drawings as your starting point and guide, in which case please do so. However, as this is our first project, it would be wise to keep the design as simple as possible. Whether you are using your own source material or whether you are using mine, we shall all proceed in exactly the same way.

THE SELECTION FOR THE DESIGN

Fig. 3 shows part of a cluster of primroses which grows on the mossy banks in my garden. It was necessary for me to select one part from the whole array of primroses to portray in my drawing. Just as the camera lens selects, so our own eyes select what to see from the entire panorama of the world around us. Choosing what to include in our picture, and deciding what to exclude from it, are early and important decisions in design processes. Some people consider what to leave out is perhaps even more important than what to put in!

Fig. 4 is the pattern derived from the original drawing. Notice that another selection process has taken place. Because this is our first project, I decided to reduce the amount of primroses to as few as possible without it becoming too simplistic. A useful way of selecting which particular part of a subject will be most suitable for a balanced design is to use a viewfinder (Fig. 5). This is made by cutting two right-angled 'corners' from card or stiff paper. It gives us the opportunity to select from a number of possibilities in terms of which particular part to choose from a larger whole, and also what kind of rectangle to have by shifting the 'corners' up and down or from side to side. The examples given in Fig. 5 indicate the possibilities of variation by this means, compared to the limitations of a

3. Primroses, *1993. Coloured pencil drawing.*

viewfinder already fixed as *one* rectangle.

Those of you who are making a selection from your own pictures might like to put into practice the following procedures as you work. First, do the 'Golden Cord' exercise (see page 6) so that your mind is unimpeded by trivia and thus more able to concentrate on the task at hand. Display all your pictures in front of you on a table which is clear of any other objects. Guided by your instinct only, choose one that you find attractive and pleasing and put all the others to one side. You will discover that if you like a project in the first instance, that incentive will carry you through any subsequent problems that may arise later on. It will be like the wind of inspiration

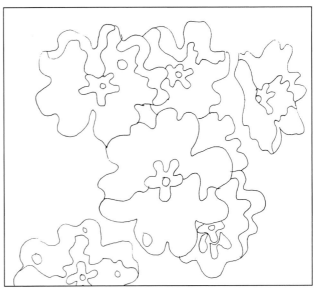

4. *Paper pattern for the* Primroses *project.*

5. The advantageous use of a viewfinder.

guiding you through the vicissitudes of your voyage of discovery!

With the help of your viewfinder, look for a number of alternative 'views' (see Fig. 5). Spend a few minutes doing this, then choose one view. Once again, rely on your instinct for your choice, but also be mindful of the following considerations. Choose a section which does not include too many primroses. Try not to mind if some are cut off at the edges; the suggestion that a design is part of a greater whole or a larger continuum can add a subtle mystery to the composition. There are only six primroses in Fig. 4 and only three of them are complete. One is cut off at the bottom, two are overlapped by the

others. It is helpful to choose a part which has a clear distinction between the tonal values and also between the colours. Notice that the green in Fig. 3 is very dark, and the shadow in the yellow is not as dark as the green; it is distinct from the green, but also dark enough to contrast with the pale yellow.

Take a little time and trouble over this selection process. Avoid the extremes of being hasty or dithering. If you are too hasty, you are likely to make mistakes; if you take too long, you are likely to give yourself too many choices and you could get unnecessarily muddled. This usually leads to headaches and bad temper, which are alien to the creative spirit and to be avoided at all cost! So enjoy the selection process but in a manner which is circumspect. It was Thomas Carlyle who described genius as 'the transcendent capacity of taking trouble, first of all'.

Eyes, ears are old. But not the sense of spring.
Look, listen, live, some inward watcher warns.
Absorb his moment's meaning: and be wise
With hearts whom the first primrose purifies.

Siegfried Sassoon, Another Spring

MAKING THE PAPER PATTERN

Once the selection has been made, we are ready to make the paper pattern. Cut a rectangle from a sheet of tracing paper so that it is exactly the same shape and size as the one formed by your viewfinder's final selection. Place it over the chosen section of the picture and, with a fine pen or pencil, trace the main contours. We need to make the pattern as simple as possible, without making it simplistic. In order to preserve the characteristics of the primroses, the delineation of the lines needs to be carefully drawn. If we draw a mere approximation of the contours, the result may be something vague and amorphous rather than these delicately formed flowers. Fig. 4 shows a definite distinction between the areas which are pale yellow (the petals in sunlight), dark yellow (the petals in shadow), the small orange-yellow (the centre of the primroses) and green (leaves and grass). Because all these areas will be cut out at some point, each line needs to be joined to another line so that they form self-contained shapes. The reason the area of green was left blank was because the same area in the drawing has a limited range of colour and tone. This was deliberate in order to act as a foil to the flowers and not to detract from their complexity. The same consideration needs to be emulated in the pattern. Always remember it is our friend and not a task-master! We need to include what is essential as exactly and as carefully as possible, and to exclude anything irrelevant. We do not want to complicate things unnecessarily!

The size of my pattern is A5, 150mm (6in) high × 210mm (8in) wide. As this is our first project, this size is just about right, neither too large nor too small. If it were too large it would take too long, which could also be the case if it were too small because of the very fine detailing that would necessitate. There are occasions when it is necessary to enlarge a pattern, for example, if you are working from a small section of a photograph or magazine cutting. Conversely, if you are deriving your pattern from a huge poster, you may need to reduce it. In either event, take it along to the nearest establishment with a photocopier, and enlarge or reduce your pattern to the size you want.

Whether you are using my pattern or making your own, you will need several copies of the same pattern. The process runs more smoothly if we use a different copy of the same pattern at each stage of the project.

SELECTING THE FABRICS

If you have never made a fabric collage before, fabric scraps may be in short supply. What you need to do is visit all your friends who have ever been involved with dressmaking or tailoring, and ask for all their offcuts. Professional tailors and dressmakers may give you their remnants too. Take a large bag, like a black dustbin liner, and come home when it is brimful and not before! You could also visit jumble sales and charity shops. Nearly thirty years ago I started by buying old clothes, curtains and bedspreads. In a very short time, and without spending much, I had accumulated a large amount of various kinds of fabrics in a number of different colours and tones.

We now need to choose the particular colours for the fabric collage. If you refer back to the last section, you will see that there are four main colour areas: pale yellow, dark yellow, orange-yellow and green. However, such descriptions are too vague; we need to be more precise.

Follow these instructions for the four colours:

1. The pale yellow, which represents the primrose petals in sunlight, is biased slightly towards green. Choose two or three different kinds of fabric in order to give variety within this limited range of colour.

2. The dark yellow, which represents the primrose petals in shadow, could present a problem. However, remember that problems are opportunities for creative development! If you look at the original drawing (Fig. 3), you will notice that the petals in shadow have been represented by a mixture of green, blue and orange strokes of the pencils. As the fabric collage develops and proceeds to the machine and hand embroidery stages, it will be possible to use all these colours. For the time being, we shall use as a foundation some mid-toned brown and purple fabrics. Such a choice may seem strange at the moment, but you will soon discover that dark yellow is often perceived as brown and sometimes purple! Select some various browns and purples of a mid-tone, neither too dark nor too light — maybe a patterned fabric composed of these two colours.

3. The orange-yellow represents the splashes of colour on the petals towards the centres of the flowers. These are sometimes in shadow as well as in sunlight. For the same reason as before, select some orange-brown fabric as well as some orange-yellow fabric. These areas are the smallest in the picture, so you only need small amounts of fabric.

4. The green represents the leaves and stalks. This is the largest area within the picture and, although the range of colour and tone is limited, the variation of colour within that limitation is considerable. Therefore, seek as many different kinds of dark green fabrics as you can. Choose shiny as well as matt, rough as well as smooth, transparent as well as opaque. Of these dark green colours, find some blue-greens as well as yellow-greens; choose some greens which seem very bright, in spite of their being a dark tone, and others which are dull. Employ this kind of variety of fabrics for all four colour categories.

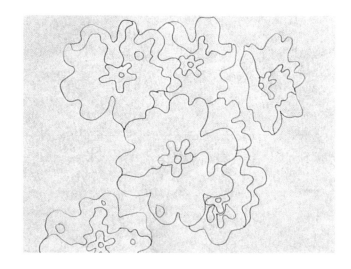

6. *The paper pattern for the* Primroses *project laid on the green hessian backing fabric.*

You can even choose patterned fabrics as long as the tonal range is not too pronounced or one colour is not particularly dominant. For example, you could use a dominantly green fabric with small areas of navy blue, dark brown and dull purple.

Finally we need to choose the best fabric for the backing material for our collage. I have found that hessian is very serviceable. It is strong enough for a sewing machine to stitch through without having to resort to a hoop or frame. It is also woven in such a way that the warp and the weft are not too close to each other, which means you can push a needle through it quite easily to apply fabric when the hand embroidery stage is reached. To a certain extent, the colour of the hessian is important. It helps to choose a colour which is dominant in the picture. In Fig. 6, you can see that I have chosen a green colour because green is the dominant colour in my original drawing and in my subsequent translation of it into fabric collage, and machine and hand embroidery. However, do not be unduly perturbed if you can only find hessian in its natural light brown colour. It will be perfectly possible to cover the entire backing fabric at the fabric collage stage. Otherwise, you could dye or paint the hessian green beforehand. You could even use another kind of fabric, but do remember it is important to select a firm fabric for the technical reasons I have just mentioned.

The background fabric needs to be 115-150mm (4-6in) larger than the paper pattern, for two reasons. It is necessary to have a margin round the edge of the picture so that it can be turned when the embroidery is finished in order to stretch it. The other reason is that embroidery, particularly machine embroidery, is a 'shrinking' process. It is helpful to remember this when you want to make a picture of a specific size.

Finally, to prevent the hessian fraying, sew round the edges with a wide zigzag stitch on the sewing machine. Once more, allow me to emphasize how important it is for you to spend your time wisely in this kind of preparation.

STARTING AND COMPLETING THE FABRIC COLLAGE STAGE

The first thing to remember is to prepare *oneself*. Therefore engage in an exercise like the 'Golden Cord' (see page 6). Then, in this calm but alert state of mind, prepare the following equipment:
1. A clear working surface
2. A comfortable, upright chair
3. Fabric scraps set out in piles of the four main colours:
    (a) pale yellow
    (b) mid-toned browns and purples
    (c) orange-yellows and orange-browns
    (d) dark greens
4. Two pairs of scissors, a pair for cutting paper and a pair for cutting fabric; take care to keep them separate because cutting paper blunts the blades!
5. Firm backing fabric, such as hessian, in green
6. Two or three copies of the paper pattern (Fig. 4), or of the one you have made yourself
7. PVA glue, dispensed into a small screwtop jar
8. A small, inexpensive brush
9. The source material (Fig. 3) or a picture you have chosen yourself

You are now ready to start the first episode of the fabric collage stage of the *Primroses* project. Begin by placing the green backing fabric on the surface of your working table and around it lay out your piles of different-coloured fabric scraps, so that they are within reach. Position one copy of the paper pattern on the backing fabric (Fig. 6) and put the others to one side for the time being. Nearby place both pairs of scissors, the brush and the jar of glue.

Start with the pile of pale yellow fabrics. This colour plays an important role in the picture and will immediately contrast with the dark green backing fabric. If you are left-handed, put the glue and the brush on the left of the hessian; if you are right-handed, put all your equipment on the right side. Attention to such small and seemingly insignificant details will help the smooth running of the activity.

From the paper pattern, cut out all those pieces which represent the pale yellow areas in the picture. Use these pieces as templates and pin them to the pale yellow fabric. If you have more than one kind of pale yellow fabric, try to use each kind more than once so that the eye is gently guided through the picture. You will soon discover that repetition is an important element in creating a harmonious balance in composition.

Likewise, if you pin the templates on the fabric so that some match the weave as well as its bias, repeat both ways more than once. In this particular project it will not matter which way the fabric scraps are applied to the backing fabric; any puckering that might occur will be rectified by the large amount of machine and hand embroidery we shall be doing later on.

Place the remaining part of the paper pattern on the backing fabric. This will now act as a stencil and will help you to place each piece of fabric in position. Cut round each template and place each piece of fabric accordingly. Before you fix the pieces of fabric in position with glue, pass your eyes over the composition to assess the balance. Be guided by your instinct in this. If you decide to alter or change anything at this stage, then do so immediately. Try to avoid dithering about whether you *should* do it or not; rely on your intuition.

> *Instinct preceded wisdom*
> *Even in the wisest men, and may sometimes*
> *Be much the better guide.*

George Lillo

Secure each piece of yellow fabric in position with tiny specks of glue on the reverse. Keep the rest of the paper pattern in position to ensure the correct placement of the yellow fabric. Figs. 7 and 8 illustrate the process and the end of this stage. Do not be unduly worried if some spots of glue show through, as sometimes happens when the fabric is very thin. All that has occurred is that the fabric has slightly darkened, which can often be put to good use! The fabric can be deliberately mottled to yield an interesting dappled effect. If the darkened effect is not suitable, it can be rectified by another layer of thicker fabric or subsequent stitching. It might be wise not to cause mistakes through lack of care and attention, but it could be equally wise to pause and reflect on such mistakes to see whether they can be put to positive use. Indeed, Edward John Phelps said, 'The man who makes no mistakes does not usually make anything.' Here is an excellent opportunity to put such a mistake to good use.

In the original drawing (Fig. 3), I have attempted to portray dewdrops on some of the petals. In order to do this, it was necessary to darken the dewdrops slightly at the bottom. The drawing is also intended to portray the dappled sunlight catching the tips of the petals bright and early on an April morning. The primroses are depicted as having this rather strong contrast of light and shadow in amongst their petals. Therefore, this darkening effect may be rather useful in helping to create the illusion of dewdrops and dappled sunshine.

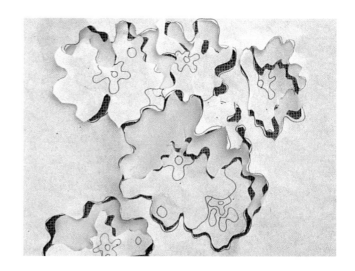

7. *Using the templates from the paper pattern.*
8. *The result of using the templates to represent the light on the primroses.*

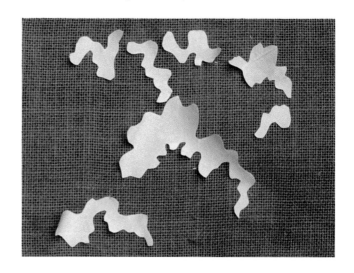

> *Glory be to God for dappled things —*
> *For skies as couple-coloured as a brindled cow;*
> *For rose-moles all in stipple upon trout that swim;*
> *Fresh-firecoal chestnut-falls; finches' wings;*
> *Landscape plotted and pieced — fold, fallow and*
> * plough*

Gerard Manley Hopkins, *Pied Beauty*

The reason for having several copies of the paper pattern is because it can be difficult to know what each piece of paper represents if some has already been cut away. Take another

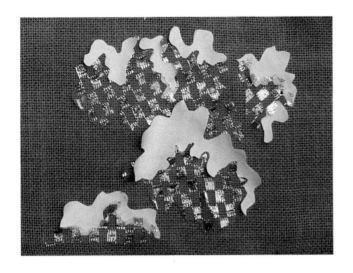

copy and cut out all those pieces which represent the areas with the primroses in shadow. Turn now to your pile of mid-toned brown and purple fabrics and proceed in the same manner as before. Fig. 9 shows this stage completed. You will also see that the brown and purple colours are contained in one fabric! If you have patterned fabric, use it to this kind of advantage.

Fig. 10 illustrates the next and final episodes of the collage stage of this project. The very small orange-yellow pieces of fabric, which represent the splashes on the petals towards the centre of the flowers, have been carefully cut and

9. *The primroses represented in light and shadow.*
10. *The collage stage of the* Primroses *project completed.*

11. Spring-time Landscape by Miranda Brookes, early 1990s. Mixed embroidery techniques. Photograph by Miranda Brookes.

positioned. The dark green fabrics, which represent the leaves and stalks, have been cut and assembled so that no one leaf or stalk appears too prominent. You will remember that we investigated this area of colour when we were discussing the paper pattern. It is just as necessary now, as it was then, to preserve the simplicity of this area so that it acts as a foil to the flowers and does not detract from their complexity.

I have mentioned before the importance of relying on your own intuition and instinct. However, I know from personal experience how difficult it is to *believe* your intuition and instinct is right! This is why I have given a few 'strict' rules about what colours and tones of fabric to position in certain places in a certain order. We

all need guidelines or rules to follow, but we must also learn that following such guidelines and rules are not the limits of our capabilities.

TIME TO PAUSE FOR RESTFUL THOUGHT

'A change is as good as a rest' and there are many times during a project when it is helpful to direct our minds to something restful but illuminating, calm but edifying, quiet yet stimulating.

We are then able to return to our former activity with renewed spirit.

Let us focus on one particular concept which has emerged several times so far. Simplicity is a term that can often be misunderstood. My use of the word refers to that quality which preserves all of the important essentials and removes unnecessary clutter. This is not easy to achieve in embroidery and I admit I have sometimes been guilty of misapplication by inverting the

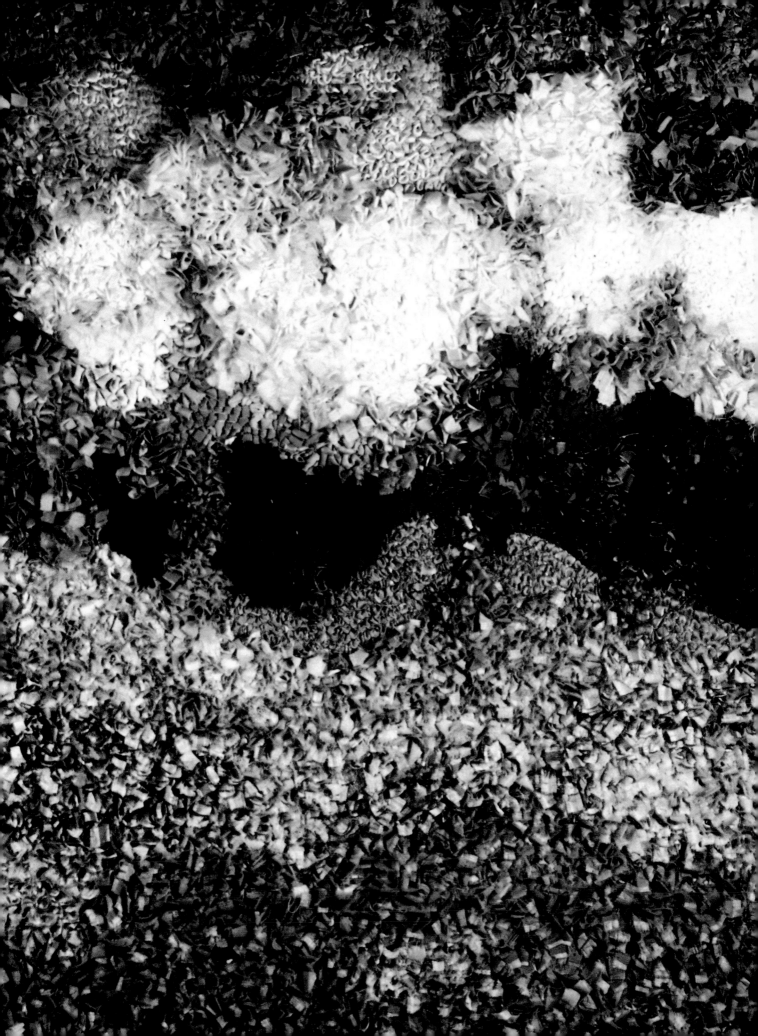

process, resulting in a mass of clutter with no essential form or meaning whatsoever!

Simplicity is not an end in art, but one arrives at simplicity in spite of oneself, in approaching the real sense of things. Simplicity is complexity itself.

Constantin Brancusi

Miranda Brookes is someone whose work I admire for its quiet simplicity and for those very qualities which we have been discussing. This is exemplified in Fig. 11, a field of young green corn in springtime. The gently flowing lines, clearly and simply delineated forms and soft, sensitive colours richly evoke the promise of new life and bright expectations. It is also a picture which suggests how nature works best in repose.

Yes, while on earth a thousand discords ring,
Man's senseless uproar mingling with his toil,
Still do thy sleepless ministers move on,
Their glorious tasks in silence perfecting;
Still working, blaming still our vain turmoil;
Labourers that shall not fail, when Man is gone.

Matthew Arnold, *Quiet Work*

Audrey Walker is another embroiderer whose work I like very much for similar reasons, even though the style and character are quite different. *Pear Blossom* (Fig. 12) is exuberance personified, typifying the gorgeous abundance of nature in springtime. The portrayal of exuberance is imparted mainly by the flamboyant textures created by the Cumberland rag rug technique. At the same time, the soft and gentle colours evoke the fragile grace of blossom petals.

Eirian Short's work has always been a source of great inspiration to me. Her embroidery *Spring*

12. Pear Blossom by Audrey Walker, mid-1970s. Cumberland rag rug technique. Photograph by Audrey Walker.

(Fig. 13) is immensely complex. Nevertheless, as Brancusi said, 'Simplicity is complexity itself,' and if one examines the picture closely it is possible to detect the careful delineation of all the forms. Each colour and tone has been so precisely articulated that one simple image has been formed in a statement of great complexity. Thus combined, simplicity and complexity create the glorious illusion of how a hawthorn tree 'flings its gorgeous drapery' around the Welsh valleys of Eirian's homeland.

Fair pledges of a fruitful tree,
Why do ye fall so fast?
Your date is not so past
But you may stay yet here awhile
To blush and gently smile
And go at last.

Robert Herrick, *To Blossoms*

Although the character and personality of these textile artists' work is quite different, all three have employed clear and simple forms as if to contain nature's energy. However, such discipline manifests, and even amplifies, the energy depicted as well as holding the forces in perfect equilibrium.

Now we are ready to return to our project after this rest. I hope you feel refreshed, invigorated, still full of the joys of spring and ready to continue!

THE FIRST MACHINE EMBROIDERY STAGE

First of all, ensure that your mind is in a state of repose and your body posture is alert and upright. Your 'Golden Cord' may have slipped once or twice, so ensure that it is in place and that both body and mind are simultaneously restful and attentive.

In this condition, clear the surface of the working table of unnecessary clutter and prepare the following:
1. The fabric collage

13. Spring by Eirian Short, 1991. Hand embroidery.
Photograph by Eirian Short.

2. A range of yellow, purple, brown and green machine embroidery and sewing threads
3. An electric sewing machine which will either lower its 'feed' or has a plate that will cover it.

You will need a darning foot that, with the 'feed' out of action, will facilitate free embroidery without having to use a hoop or frame to hold the fabric tight. (This assumes you are using a firm fabric, such as hessian.)

Clip on the darning foot and insert a fairly thick needle, about 90 or 100. Then drop or cover the 'feed'. Set the stitch length to zero. Although this is temporarily out of commission, by virtue of the 'feed' being lowered or covered, it is important to keep it from moving in order to save unnecessary wear and tear on your machine. Now set the stitch width to the widest zigzag which your machine permits. The wider the stitches, the more efficient they are in sewing the applied fabric to the backing material. It is possible, of course, to vary the stitch width from the widest zigzag to a straight running stitch and each variation will create its own particular effect, but as this is our first project together let us use the same stitch width for the time being.

Choose a pale yellow thread to start with, to follow the same sequence of colours that we used in the fabric collage stage. Wind the same colour thread on to your spool or bobbin. Machine embroidery experts recommend the same colour below as above, but not necessarily the same thread. In order to preserve the smooth action of the machine, it is wiser to have a cotton thread wound onto the bobbin all the time, because some other threads (particularly some synthetic ones) have a habit of slipping and producing irregularities. In spite of diligently following all the tension adjustment instructions in the sewing machine manual, you may not achieve perfect stitches all the time, hence the reason for having the same colour thread above as well as below. Although such 'mistakes' can produce interesting results and can be employed usefully in ways we have recently discussed, I should not confuse you with too many possibilities at this stage!

Before you start to sew the fabric collage, practise on a spare piece of hessian backing fabric to ensure that you have adjusted the tension correctly, that the movement is smooth and easy and that you are happy with this arrangement. Stitch the pale yellow cotton across and around all the pieces of fabric of this colour and tone. At this stage, sew sparingly; only a few stitches are needed to secure the fabric pieces to the backing.

14. *The first machine embroidery stage of the* Primroses *project.*

You can also take this thread onto other parts of the picture. The following guide applies to any thread, whether you are sewing by machine or by hand. It has become almost an absolute rule for me during recent years. For 90 per cent of the area within the picture, stitch each coloured thread on the fabric of the same *colour* and *tone*. In this instance, the pale yellow thread needs to be stitched to the pale yellow fabric. For 5 per cent of the area, it is possible to stitch this thread on any other coloured fabric as long as it is *the same tone*. For instance, if there are some glittering green fabrics in the area that represents the stalks and leaves in your collage, you could use some pale yellow thread on these fabrics because when they reflect light they have *the same pale tone*. In Fig. 14 a mid- to dark-toned green thread, which had been travelling on fabric of the same colour and tone, has also been travelling on the mid- to dark-toned purple and brown fabric — sparingly, just for 5 per cent. For the last 5 per cent, any thread can be made to travel across any fabric of any colour and any tone. However, please remember that it is only 5 per cent! Curiously enough, it is this last 5 per cent where colours and tones are contrasted rather than matched which invigorates the life of the embroidery.

There is measure in everything. There are fixed limits, beyond which and short of which, right cannot find a resting place.

Horace

Follow this guide with whatever threads you decide to use in this machine embroidery stage of your project. Return to some threads which you have used before, so that your earlier sparing use may become fuller and richer, or left sparse in areas, just as you wish. Keep the original source material close at hand so that you can refer to it from time to time. In my drawings of the primroses, you will notice some distinctly blue strokes of the pencil in the dark green areas (Fig. 3). This is because blue, together with yellow, is a component of green and therefore can be used in the embroidery. Fig. 14 shows the completion of this machine embroidery stage; notice some stitching in amongst the green area made with blue thread.

Although I have given you some guidelines and a few rules to help you, also important is *your* choice of colour and tone, and where you place these in your embroidery. Furthermore, the way you direct your sewing stitches is as much part of the construction as everything else. So once more I urge you to rely on your feelings, instinct and intuitive judgement.

THE HAND EMBROIDERY STAGE

Machine embroidery can integrate the fabric collage pieces very satisfactorily. It can help to create a harmonious unity by softening abrupt edges, modulating sudden changes of colour and tone, and transforming what might have been rather crude at an earlier stage to something more subtle and graceful. In spite of such virtues, machine embroidery can nullify an earlier and often more interesting textural variety. Often it happens that where there is a gain, there is also a loss. However, all is not completely lost. Hand embroidery can reinstate such

15. *The hand embroidery stage of the* Primroses *project.*

varieties of texture.

Your choice of threads for this stage can be as varied as you like. Try using weaving and knitting yarns as well as traditional embroidery wools, cottons and silks. Select as many colours as you like within the same range as before. If you look at Fig. 15, you will see a variety of different thicknesses and textures of threads have been used, including pale yellow parcel string found in a local street market! It has a wonderfully glossy sheen and is able to create the effect of dappled sunlight that I wanted to achieve. Embroidery has been described as the embellishment of a surface; I also want my stitches to construct the form of the picture as well as decorate it.

Look again at Fig. 15 and you will notice that only straight stitch has been used. Within its limitations, straight stitch offers quite a large range; it can be worked in any direction and at any length. The constructive element of my stitches is concerned with their direction, and is chosen for three main reasons. First, the outward movement within the primroses themselves is to portray them like stars exploding with light, which is how I was beginning to *feel* them emotionally rather than *see* them. Second, I deliberately directed a sweeping movement of stitchery in the area which represents the leaves and stalks in order to evoke the illusion of a gentle morning breeze. Finally, the various directions — some repeated, others contrasted — are deliberately positioned to maintain a balanced harmony throughout the composition.

Try this kind of hand stitching, directing it in as many ways as you deem fit. Keep the original source material by you so that you can refer to it from time to time. Remember it is there as a guide; if your desire is to direct your stitches according to your feelings, then do so.

Heroism feels and never reasons.

Ralph Waldo Emerson

THE SECOND MACHINE EMBROIDERY STAGE AND CONCLUSION OF THE PROJECT

My assessment of my hand stitching was that, although it partly achieved what I had intended, it seemed rather too prominent in the design as a whole. Figs. 16 and 17 illustrate the final stage of the project. I decided to return the embroidery to the sewing machine and to sew over the hand embroidery with straight stitching. This couching technique brought all the elements of the design together, and created the desired bal-

16. *The second machine embroidery stage of the* Primroses *project.*

ance and harmony throughout the composition.

When you have completed the hand embroidery stage, look at your picture to see whether you also find a similar unresolved aspect within the design. If so, try the couching technique with the sewing machine; if you set the dial or button to straight stitch, you will find it very much like drawing with a needle.

RECAPITULATION AND CONSOLIDATION

For the rest of this chapter we shall revise and consolidate what we have started to learn, rather than trying any new techniques. We shall remain with the same techniques of fabric collage, machine and hand embroidery but shall explore new ways of using them.

Choose subjects like animals or birds as well as floral themes; select a different format for the picture, vertical instead of horizontal; try cutting the fabric in different ways, for example, very small random pieces composed to form a shape; and explore other colour schemes and tonal organization. In short, try *new methods* of exploring the *same technique*. Be patient in your practice and you will find that all kinds of possibilities will emerge.

Patience is a necessary ingredient to genius.

Benjamin Disraeli

Some of the embroidery pictures shown here are deliberately different in subject matter. I am particularly delighted to include Rita Marsland's *Lambing in the Barn* (Fig. 18), which she started on one of my weekend courses and finished at home. I am including a number of students' work in this book to demonstrate that everyone can attempt the methods and techniques I show you, and can do so splendidly.

Sensitivity to Nature must come first: technique does not matter.

Paul Cézanne

17. *The* Primroses *project completed.*

18. Lambing in the Barn *by Rita Marsland, 1991.*
Fabric collage with machine and hand embroidery.
Photograph by Rita Marsland.

19. Violets, *1993. Fabric collage with machine and hand embroidery.*

I know a bank where the wild thyme blows
Where oxlips and the nodding violet grows.

William Shakespeare, *A Midsummer Night's Dream*

The reason for showing you different subjects in the same technique is to dismiss the erroneous idea that certain materials and techniques are more suitable for particular subjects than others. Cézanne (see page 27) implies that it does not matter which technique is employed as long as nature is allowed to direct. For our purposes, 'nature' can be understood to include the nature of light and colour in our fabric and thread as well as the nature of light and colour in the countryside and the seasons. Thus the 'nature' of our materials will direct and inform the 'nature' of the techniques we choose to employ.

In order for us to develop our sensitive under-standing of the nature of the materials we use and the techniques we employ, we all need to practise *regularly and constantly*. It is by such means that we shall develop the skills of the craftsperson within us, and also open up the eyes of the artist who is part of our creative being.

Constant practice often excels even talent.

Cicero

20. The Rabbit, *1993. Fabric collage with machine
and hand embroidery.*

Eternity of Nature

*All Nature has a feeling: woods, fields, brooks
Are life eternal; and in silence they
Speak happiness beyond the reach of books;
There's nothing mortal in them; their decay
Is the green life of change; to pass away
And come again in blooms revivified.
Its birth was heaven, eternal is its stay,
And with the sun and moon shall still abide
Beneath their day and night and heaven wide.*

John Clare

21. The Snail and Celandine, *1993. Fabric collage
with machine and hand embroidery.*

22. The Thrush's Nest, *1993. Fabric collage with
machine and hand embroidery.*

The Thrush's Nest

*Within a thick and spreading hawthorn bush
That overhung a mole-hill large and round,
I heard from morn to morn a merry thrush
Sing hymns to sunrise, and I drank the sound
With joy; and, often an intruding guest,
I watched her secret toils from day to day —
How true she warped the moss to form a nest,
And modelled it within the wood and clay;
And by and by, like heath-bells gilt with dew,
There lay her shining eggs, as bright as flowers,
Ink-spotted over shells of greeny blue;
And there I witnessed, in the sunny hours,
A brood of Nature's minstrels chirp and fly,
Glad as that sunshine and the laughing sky.*

John Clare

*23. Cowslips, 1993. Fabric collage with machine and
hand embroidery.*

> *The cowslips tall her pensioners be;*
> *In their gold coats spots you see;*
> *Those be rubies, fairy favours,*
> *In their freckles live their savours.*
> *I must go and seek some dewdrops here,*
> *And hang a pearl in every cowslip's ear.*

William Shakespeare, *A Midsummer Night's Dream*

CHAPTER TWO

Summer

If we had never before looked upon the earth, but suddenly came to it man or woman grown, set down in the midst of a summer mead, would it not seem to us a radiant vision? The hues, the shapes, the song and life of birds, above all the sunlight, the breath of heaven, resting on it; the mind would be filled with its glory, unable to grasp it.

Richard Jeffries, *The Open Air*

Summer is the season when the fresh promises of spring reach a particularly luxuriant stage. Flowers are in abundance and everywhere the air becomes heavy with their perfume. On a summer day, you might find me sitting in a field of buttercups painting the view or a detail of the surrounding hedgerow entwined with woodbine and sweet eglantine. At such times work and holiday form one holy day, filled with wonder at nature's glory.

There are two main projects in this chapter, both developments of what we have learned in Chapter One. Both include fabric collage methods and machine and hand embroidery techniques, and both follow the same order and procedure. However, you will discover new and different methods and techniques to improve your prowess.

24. May Blossom, 1993. Fabric collage with machine and hand embroidery. Photograph by Ashton James.

The Buttercup Field

When daisies pied and violets blue,
And lady-smocks all silver-white,
And cuckoo-buds of yellow hue
Do paint the meadows with delight.

William Shakespeare, *Love's Labours Lost*

THE INSPIRATION

Daisies and buttercups are for many of us a reminder of our childhood, when we enjoyed the delight of rambling through the long grass and brilliantly coloured flowers. Shakespeare's name for the buttercup is 'cuckoo-bud'. You can imagine how he saw a meadow full of early summer flowers and painted it in words, as we shall now 'paint' such a meadow with fabric and thread.

Fig. 25 is one of many studies I made this year of a particular field of buttercups alongside the River Wye near my home in Herefordshire. It was the brilliance of the flowers' yellow hues which first attracted my attention. As I began to paint, their profusion took on the appearance of a glittering tapestry carpeting the graceful undulations of the field. In this amazing tapestry it was possible to detect all the colours of the rainbow, for in amongst the yellow buttercups were tall green grasses, blue speedwell, purple and white clovers, orange lady's slipper and scarlet pimpernel. I was able to sit there all day long with the sunshine gleaming around me and the soft breezes warming my cheeks and bringing the skylark's song to my ears, and I knew that spring had passed into summer. There were enormous problems with all the paintings I made of this field, but it was good to remember the 'Golden Cord' (see page 6) and to take frequent rests, often by walking round the field, before returning to the task refreshed and renewed. When the day's work was done, it was important to complete the activity in quiet repose as evening came, and to watch the field grow still and quiet.

USING AND SELECTING THE SOURCES OF INSPIRATION

If you wish to use another picture of a buttercup field, then please do so. You may like to use a photograph which you have taken yourself, or you may have discovered something in a magazine or a calendar. If you have found a number of different sources, it is always a good idea to spread them all out before you and then decide speedily and by instinct which one appeals most to you.

You will remember that in Chapter One we also employed the aid of a viewfinder, especially if the original picture was rather too complicated and it was necessary to select a small section from the larger whole. If you decide to follow my painting (Fig. 25), you could use either the entire composition or just a part of it for this project. I shall be dealing with the entire composition. Whichever picture or section of a picture you choose to use, we shall all follow the same procedure.

Before we make a paper pattern, I want to make one rather important point. Some people have the strange idea that it is cheating to have the original source close at hand throughout the creative process! Other people declare, 'It's in my head.' However, you should always put your design on paper first, because it helps the procedure later on. It is important to have a clear idea in your head before the pattern is made, just as it is before a photograph is taken or a picture painted. The use of the viewfinder helps to clarify muddled thinking, and guides us towards knowing what we are about to do before we do it. Remember that this 'knowing' is still only a guide and does not preclude changes and developments as the project progresses.

25. The Buttercup Field, *1992. Watercolour and gouache painting.*

Always think your design out in your head before you begin to get it on paper. Don't begin by slobbering and messsing about in the hope that something may come out of it. You must see it before you can draw it, whether the design is yours or Nature's.

William Morris, 'Art and Beauty of the Earth'

MAKING THE PAPER PATTERN

Using a photocopying machine is very helpful. Not only does it enlarge or reduce the original source material to a suitable-sized pattern for our textile pictures, it also enables us to see the tonal values of the original picture more clearly. Very often we can be so beguiled by the vividness of a dark purple or the brightness of a mid-toned red that we think the tonal values of these colours are paler than they actually are. By removing the colour, the tonal values of the shapes are emphasized; this helps us to see the simplicity in the complexity, so that we can draw the most essential contours for the pattern.

Fig. 26 is a reduced photocopy of the original painting (Fig. 25). From this I drew all of the main contours by tracing them through layout paper, and enlarged this drawing. That then became my master paper pattern (Fig. 27), 460 × 350mm (18 × 14in). I have attempted to keep my lines few and simple, so that I did

26. *Reduced photocopy of* The Buttercup Field *painting.*

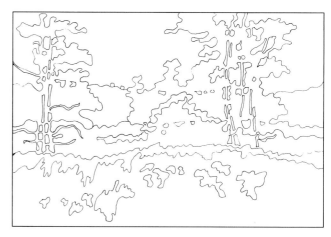

27. *Master paper pattern for* The Buttercup Field *project.*

not become ensnared by little details at an early stage. It was only necessary to draw the main areas which represent the sky, the trees' foliage and some of their trunks and branches, the distant hills, the bushes in the middle-distance and the foreground of the buttercup field itself. Although it may seem rather crude, it is important to remember that the purpose of this pattern is for locating, rather than finely delineating, these areas. The extremely complicated contours (for example, the foliage against the sky) are deliberately simple at this early stage; the minute detailing to create the delicacy of this foliage is done at the collage and embroidery stages, guided by this simple contour.

Nothing is more simple than greatness; indeed, to be simple is to be great.

Ralph Waldo Emerson, *Literary Ethics*

It is a good idea to have several copies of the same paper pattern, just as we did in the last project. Fig. 27 is the tracing from the photocopy of the painting. Fig. 28 is the same pattern, but with two main lines emphasized to denote the areas of sky and the distant hills. Fig. 29 is also the same pattern, with another two lines

emphasized: one, somewhat convoluted, represents the tops of the trees and bushes, the other represents where the lower parts of the trees and bushes 'meet' the top of the buttercup field.

Remember, paper patterns are our guides and, like rules, are intended to help us: 'Rules are for the obedience of the foolish and for the guidance of the wise.' (Anon)

SELECTING THE FABRICS

Choose a firm fabric for the backing material of the collage. I used a piece of hessian whose original dimensions were 560 × 480mm (22 × 19in), even though the final dimensions of the picture itself are 460 × 350mm (18 × 14in).

You will remember that it is necessary to allow for the 'shrinking' process that embroidery, particularly machine embroidery, causes and to ensure a margin of about 115-150mm (4-6in), so that the edges of the embroidery can be turned in in order to stretch it when it is finished. It is helpful to choose a colour which makes a contribution to the picture. My choice was green because that colour features most in the painting.

Select from your fabric scraps the same variety and kinds of material as we used before (see

28. *Paper pattern, emphasizing the areas representing the sky and distant hills.*

29. *Paper pattern, emphasizing the areas representing the middle-distance trees and bushes.*

page 16). It is enormous fun to contrast different types of fabric, such as velvets, cottons and silks with nylons, polyesters and even crimplenes! Look at the painting (Fig. 25), which is acting as a guide to help you choose the colours which are needed. Obviously greens, blues and yellows are important, but there are other colours such as very pale orange, reds and purples. You will be able to detect these pale-toned colours in different parts of the picture, for example, the trunks and branches of the trees and in the field itself. Within these areas, you will also notice small vestiges of browns, dark purples and dark blues among the shadows.

Yellow is intrinsically a pale-toned colour. Nevertheless, select fabric which varies in tones within its limited tonal range and also choose a number of different *hues* of yellow: choose some 'warm' yellows, which are biased towards orange, and some 'cool' yellows, which are biased towards green. Continue this regard for hues in your selection of *all* colours. Blues and greens, whose tonal range within the picture is very extensive from pale to dark, are also extremely varied in their hues. Therefore, choose some blues which are biased towards green and some which are biased towards purple; similarly, choose some greens which

are biased towards yellow and some which are biased towards blue. Very pale reds, oranges and purples and the very dark browns and purples are small in quantity, but these small amounts of colour play an important role; it is equally important to choose a range of hues in these colours as it is with all the others. It is through the inclusion of these colours in these proportions that the vibrating quality of light may be achieved and the summer mood of our picture realized.

STARTING AND COMPLETING THE FABRIC COLLAGE STAGE

If you have forgotten all about the 'Golden Cord' (see page 6) and as a result have become rigid and tense, then practise this relaxed but attentive exercise. It is important to approach our projects in a calm but alert state of mind and body. In this condition, prepare the following equipment:

1. A working surface free of clutter
2. An upright, comfortable chair
3. Fabric scraps set out in piles of the following colours and tones:
    (a) pale-toned blues and whites

(b) mid-toned and dull-coloured blues

(c) dark blues

(d) pale to mid-toned greens

(e) mid-toned to dark greens

(f) pale reds ('pinks') and pale purples ('mauves')

(g) dark browns and dark purples

(h) yellows

NB Remember to select a large variety of hues in all these colours, as we have just discussed

4. Two pairs of scissors—a pair for cutting paper and a pair for cutting fabric

5. Firm backing fabric, such as hessian, in green

6. Your two main copies of the paper pattern (Figs. 28 and 29) or several copies of the one you have made yourself

7. Some PVA glue, dispensed into a small screw-top jar

8. A small, inexpensive brush

9. The source material (Fig. 25) or a picture you have chosen yourself

First sew round the edges of the hessian to prevent them fraying using a wide zigzag stitch on the sewing machine.

Now you are ready to begin the collage stage of this project. Start by placing the green backing fabric on the working surface in front of you. On this place one copy of your paper pattern (Fig. 28). On your working hand side, put the glue, the brush and the two pairs of scissors. Near these and still within reach, place the heaps of fabric scraps.

For this picture, we shall cut and assemble the fabric scraps in a different way to our first project. We shall also use the pattern in a slightly different way. As we cut out each section of the pattern, we are not going to use it as a template as we did before. Instead we shall throw each section away and use the remainder of the pattern as a stencil. The green backing fabric revealed by the absence of the section of paper we have just thrown away will be constructed with very small and seemingly randomly cut pieces of fabric. In fact, if you look at Fig. 30 you will see that the collage is not dissimilar to a mosaic in its construction.

Cut away the whole of the top section of the pattern along the dark line which represents where the sky 'meets' the top of the distant hills. This line passes through the trees in the middle distance, but do not worry about this; we shall assemble the green areas (the trees), *on top of* the blue-and-white area we are now about to assemble (the sky). Place the remainder of the paper pattern on top of the hessian.

Now cut the pale blue and the white fabric into very small pieces, no bigger than the size of your little fingernail. However, within the range of this small dimension, vary the size of the pieces, making some smaller than others. Furthermore, vary the cutting edge so that some of your pieces have straight edges, some curved edges and some both straight and curved edges. In this way, it is possible to create subtle interest by very simple means. Put each fabric in a separate pile, just as a painter squeezes small amounts of different hues of the one colour separately on his palette. It will not be necessary to use very much of any one kind of fabric because of the large variety you have selected. Check the area of the green hessian onto which you are about to apply these small pieces and match it with the amount you are cutting. If you cut too many, you may find that you need them in other parts of your picture later on, or you can always store them in plastic bags ready for another picture.

Take up some of the glue with the brush, and with *this* pick up one of the tiny fabric pieces and stick it on the hessian, within the area which is to represent the sky. Continue to do this with several pieces from the same pile of fabric, dispersing them over different parts of the same area. Then select another pile and proceed in the same manner. Continue in this way until several pieces from all the piles have been used and the hessian is covered with fabric. If you find that some of the pale blue fabric is rather too dark a

30. *The collage stage of* The Buttercup Field *project. The detail (left) shows the very small pieces of fabric used to construct the collage.*

31. Hayfield *by Eirian Short, 1981. Hand
embroidery. Photograph by Eirian Short.*

tone to represent the sky, substitute these pieces
with others of a paler tone or cover them with
transparent pieces of fabric such as net, organdie
or lace.

When the area of the sky is completed, cut
away from the same copy of the paper pattern
the area which represents the distant hills by
cutting along the line where the hills 'meet' the
top of the bushes. Then select some mid-toned
blues which are also rather dull; avoid using
bright blues in this area because they may

appear to advance rather than recede. Cut these mid-toned, rather grey blues just as before and arrange them into particular coloured piles. Place the remainder of the paper pattern back on the hessian and, with the help of the brush, glue the mid-toned blue fabrics to the area of hessian which denotes the distant hills.

Remove the remainder of the paper pattern you have just been using and throw it away. Replace it with another copy (Fig. 29). To cut out the area which represents the middle-distant bushes and trees, cut along the convoluted line which represents the tops of the trees and bushes and along the line which represents where the lower parts of the trees and bushes 'meet' the field. Put it to one side, but still in your view, and place the remaining pieces of your paper pattern on the hessian, in their appropriate positions. In the original picture (Fig. 25), you can see that a lot of different colours are present in this area. To avoid confusion we shall deal with each colour, or small group of colours, in turn.

Let us begin with dark blues, dark purples and dark browns, which are to represent the trunks and branches of the trees in shadow. Select these dark-toned fabrics and cut them into short, thin strips, some curved, others straight. As before, arrange them in separate piles for different colours. In order to be as accurate as possible, you could mark on the backing fabric the lines which represent the treetrunks and branches with a fine pen or a soft, sharp-pointed pencil. Use the cut-away piece from the pattern to guide you.

Marking the backing fabric can be immensely helpful. Indeed, there was a time when I did not bother with a paper pattern at all and marked the design straight onto the hessian, guided by my eyes only. This resulted in inaccuracies which I only noticed later on and a lot of unnecessary time was spent changing everything. Furthermore, many of the guidelines were covered up at an early stage and as a result I became totally lost! Therefore, avoid substituting one procedure with another but use the benefits of both together. Once you have planned where the thin strips of dark blue, dark purple and dark brown fabrics are to be positioned, assemble them as deftly as you can with the brush and glue. Be guided by the original picture (Fig. 25). You may find that it is necessary to cut some of your strips more finely and thinly. Avoid clumsiness and awkwardness at all times; rather aspire towards grace and elegance of line in order to create the sinuous flow of the trunks and branches. Cut some pale reds ('pink') and some pale purple ('mauve') into thin strips, and assemble them in those places which represent

the lighter parts of the treetrunks and branches.

Around, and occasionally over, these strips which represent the branches we now need to assemble dark green fabric and small amounts of more dark blue, dark purple and dark brown to represent the leaves of the bushes and trees in shadow. The fabric needs to be cut even smaller than before and in more varied shapes, as the variety of pieces representing the sky. Assemble each fabric into different piles so that your use of the brush and glue is orderly and speedy. Once all this has been done, select mid- to very pale-toned greens and even some greenish yellows. Cut them as before, assemble them into orderly piles and attach them to the backing fabric next to, and occasionally over, the dark colours which represent the leaves in shadow so that you achieve the appearance of the leaves in sunlight.

Now you are ready for the area which represents the field of buttercups. This time it is not necessary to use the paper pattern because all the parts representing everything other than the field have been constructed. Therefore, the only area of green hessian remaining must represent the field. The colours needed are all yellows, all greens, some dark and mid-toned blues, a few pale reds ('pinks'), a few pale purples ('mauves') and a few dark purples. You may have some small fabric scraps left over from before which you can use. In order to create the illusion of tall grasses, cut some of the fabric into short, thin strips just as we did to represent the treetrunks and branches. Other shapes and sizes need to be cut to represent the buttercups and the other flowers and plants growing in the meadow. Keep looking at the original picture (Fig. 25) and the completed collage stage of my embroidery (Fig. 30) to help you.

Once you have completed all these areas, put the entire collage a long way from you, hold it up and look at it in the mirror and even try pinning it on your washing line so that you can see it from a distance! It is important to look at what we do from a long way away because it helps us to view it as a whole, to assess how the repre-

*32. Poppy Field by Verina Warren, 1980s. Mixed
embroidery and painting techniques. Photograph by
Verina Warren.*

sentation is realized and how the balance of all
the elements of line, tone and colour is
achieved. My assessment of the collage stage of
my embroidery was that there was too much
yellow at the bottom of the picture. Although
the illusion of masses of buttercups was
achieved, the balance of yellow worried me. In
order to rectify this, I brought some more pieces
of yellow up into the upper part of the picture
where some pale greens and greenish yellows
were representing the leaves in sunlight. This
restored the balance of yellow throughout the
picture as a whole, and enlivened the leaves on
the trees and bushes more than before. I also
noticed that the pale red and pale mauve were
creating a lively effect so I dared to incorporate

some more into the area portraying the sky,
which immediately created that warm glow you
sometimes see on summer evenings.

*Chances, as they are now called, I regard as
guidances, and even, if rightly understood,
commands, which, as far as I have read history,
the best and sincerest men think providential.*

John Ruskin

Trust to chance as your guide when you assess
your progress in this way, just as we relied on
our instinct before.

Chance fights on the side of the prudent.

Euripides

33. Grasses *by Verina Warren. Mixed embroidery*
and painting techniques. Photograph by
Verina Warren.

TIME TO PAUSE FOR RESTFUL THOUGHT

It is always a good idea to take a few rests in between each of your projects. Let us now use this opportunity by taking our minds off the problems of our work and allowing them to focus on other things for a while, so that when we return to our project we may be fortified, strengthened and refreshed.

We have already been inspired by the work of Eirian Short. Let us now look at another embroidery of hers entitled *Hayfield* (Fig. 31). Although it is entirely hand-stitched, it has a number of features which are similar to our project and from which we can learn a great deal. Notice first the importance of the stitch directions and how various they are. Not only do these gently persuasive directions convey the movement of the breeze through the hayfield and across the sky and clouds, they also give vitality to the whole scene. Then notice how many subtle hues and tones are used, particularly in the area which represents the field itself, where pale yellows, pale oranges and pale reds can be detected in amongst the browns and yellow ochres. Such hues and tones and gentle stitch direction richly evoke the atmosphere of a hot summer's afternoon.

Far off the rook, tired by the mid-day beam,
Caws lazily this summer afternoon;
The butterflies, with wandering up and down
O'er flower-bright marsh and meadow, wearied
*   seem*

Thomas Doubleday, *Summer Afternoon*

Verina Warren is an artist whose embroidery I have admired for many years. The evocation of high summer is gloriously exemplified in her portrayal of a poppy field (Fig. 32). Similar lessons to those we have learnt from Eirian Short's *Hayfield* can be learnt here. Notice how the stitch directions, which are mainly embroidered by machine, in the central sections of the picture are inclined more towards a vertical direction. This creates little movement and gives the feeling of a still, hot summer's day. However, the stitch directions are various enough to animate the surface with quiet energy. Assisting this energy is the juxtaposition of red and green; any pairing of complementary colours will create the effect of glowing vibration. Look also at the trees on the left and in some areas of the dark green corn; here you will see small quantities of blue stitching, and you can detect yellow stitches in the pale green corn and leaves. Blue and yellow are the two component primary colours which make the secondary colour green. If traces of the component primary colours are present in the secondary colour which they form, they create a vibrating effect — very evocative of high summer.

High Summer

I never wholly feel that summer is high,
However green the trees, or loud the birds,
However movelessly eye-winking herds
Stand in field ponds, or under large trees lie,
Till I do climb all cultured pastures by,
That hedged by hedgerows studiously fretted
*   trim,*
Smile like a lady's face with lace laced prim,
And on some moor or hill that seeks the sky
Lonely and nakedly, — utterly lie down,
And feel the sunshine throbbing on body and
*   limb,*
My drowsy brain in pleasant drunkenness swim,
Each rising thought sink back and dreamily
*   drown*
Smiles creep o'er my face, and smother my lips,
*   and cloy*
Each muscle sink to itself, and separately enjoy.

Ebenezer Jones

Verina Warren's embroidered picture *Grasses* (Fig. 33) is as simple as her *Poppy Field* is sumptuous. Nevertheless, within its simplicity there are many riches to be found. Within the limits of the colour there is a strong tonal contrast. The curves of the paler grasses are enhanced by the more vertical darker grasses at the top of the picture. Both examples of contrast create the illusion of depth and form within the picture, as well as suggesting gusts of wind blowing through the tufts of grass. Both this picture and that of the poppy field have borders which are painted to provide contrast with detail. Verina Warren writes, 'In design, contrasts are seen again, landscape within landscape, and season within season. Technically, developments have seen the juxtaposition of painting with embroidery and the use of silk-bound borders in linking these elements together.' Of particular interest is the idea of taking such a seemingly insignificant

detail as a tuft of grass in order to evoke generalities of great importance. It is as if the extraordinary has been discovered in the ordinary.

Even the grass its happy moment has
In May, when glistening buttercups make gold;
The exulting millions of the meadow-grass
Give out a green thanksgiving from the mould.
Even the blade that has not even a blossom
Creates a mind, its joy's persistent soul
Is a warm spirit on the old earth's bosom

John Masefield, *Look At the Grass*

Audrey Walker's work encouraged us in the previous chapter. Here is another example, a detail of *There's a Rainbow Around My Shoulder* (Fig. 34). It is one of a series of embroideries for which she used a 1930s transfer-printed tablecloth of the kind she remembers her mother and grandmother embroidering during her childhood. She writes, 'There is a great deal of love in those humble pieces and I wanted to incorporate some of this affection in my own work.' I wonder if, like me, you notice with affection how some of the different pieces of material we use bring back fond memories.

The main reason for the inclusion of this embroidery is, of course, because of its colour. Although blue and green sometimes emit a feeling of coldness, this is not so here. The blue and green are mostly of a pale tone, much white is present and so also are reds, purples, yellows and oranges in lesser quantities and in mid- to pale tones. This kind of juxtapositioning of colours, which we have just discussed in the embroideries by Verina Warren and Eirian Short,

is another example of how a glowing vibration of light may be achieved. In this particular embroidery the effect is one of brightness, freshness and joyfulness; it is just the kind of effect we can emulate in our picture of the buttercup field. Let us now return to our project fired with new enthusiasm!

THE FIRST MACHINE EMBROIDERY STAGE

This stage is very much the same as the corresponding stage in our first project. The procedure is identical, but the choice of colour threads is different.

First, ensure that your 'Golden Cord' (see page 6) is in the correct position so that your posture is upright and comfortable. This also helps the mind to be in an alert and peaceful state. Then prepare the following equipment:
1. The fabric collage
2. A range of blue, yellow, green, purple, pale red, pale orange, brown and white machine embroidery and sewing threads
3. An electric sewing machine with a darning foot clipped into place, a thick needle (90 or 100) and a 'feed' which can be lowered or covered so that you can engage in a similar kind of free-embroidery technique as before

Set the stitch length to zero and the stitch width to the widest zigzag to begin with. Later on it will be possible to try any width, but during the early part of this stage you need to fix all the tiny fabric pieces as quickly as possible and this is most efficiently done with the widest stitch.

Follow exactly the same procedure as in the first project (see page 24). Match the colour of top and bottom threads. At this early stage stitch sparingly with each colour; three or four stitches in each piece of matching material is ample. If you decide to enhance any part of your picture with more dense stitchery, it is better to do so later on in this stage. Follow the same guide as we used before to help you place each coloured thread in the picture. For 90 per cent match both colour and tone, for 5 per cent match the

34. There's a Rainbow Around My Shoulder (detail) by Audrey Walker, early 1980s. Mixed embroidery techniques. Photograph by Audrey Walker.

tones of any colour, and for the last 5 per cent mismatch any colour and tone. In this way, you can embellish and enhance the colours and tones already established by the fabric pieces, and the occasional 'mismatch' creates a link through the composition as a whole.

When every piece of collage fabric has at least one stitch in it and you have taken all your coloured threads through the picture, you may like to take some through again in order to enrich certain areas. Be guided by the original source material (Fig. 25) to see which parts need more attention. However, take care not to overdo too many areas. We still have much hand embroidery to do and it will be difficult to pass the needle through a lot of dense machine stitching. Exercise restraint and discipline in order to allow for even more sumptuous details to be included in the next two stages!

THE HAND EMBROIDERY STAGE

It is at this point that we shall employ another technique. In our first project, *Primroses*, we used long and short straight stitches. Here we shall use a method which makes a series of looped stitches. Each loop is formed by making a very small stitch like a seed stitch. However, instead of the thread being pulled tight against the surface, it is pulled through gradually so that just enough is left to form a loop. It is then secured by taking the needle back through the fabric and splitting the thread on the reverse side. The massing of such loops (which can vary in density, thickness and, to a small degree, height) enhances the texture of the embroidered surface considerably, as well as facilitating the inclusion of small details. The height of each loop can vary slightly and can be used to great advantage. A slightly higher series of stitches can complement a sequence of slightly lower stitches and cause graceful undulations. Areas in the foreground could be embellished with more prominently looped stitches than those in the distance. The thickness of each loop can be caused by either

the gauge of the thread or the number of threads used in the needle at any one time.

Choose similar colours, as you did for the first machine embroidery stage, and select many different kinds of threads, including weaving and knitting yarns as well as traditional embroidery threads. It is the variety that contributes to our enjoyment in making the embroideries in this book.

Variety is the mother of enjoyment.

Benjamin Disraeli

THE SECOND MACHINE EMBROIDERY STAGE AND CONCLUSION OF THE PROJECT

Fig. 35 shows the completed version of this project. In order to integrate the hand-embroidered loops, I used a special foot which makes machine-embroidered loops. Some sewing machines call it a 'tailor-tacking foot', others a 'fringe foot'. Clip this foot onto your machine and bring up (or uncover) the 'feed'. The stitch length as well as the stitch width needs to be in operation for this process. Set the needle position either to the left or right, because the process begins and ends with a straight stitch to secure the loop. The length of the stitch can vary as you wish, according to the needs of the embroidery.

If you have never used this sort of foot before, practise on a spare length of hessian or some other kind of firm fabric. Begin with three or four close, straight stitches. Stop and set the stitch width to the widest zigzag. Turn the wheel by hand to check that the needle is clearing the flange on the foot and that the top tension is correct. If the bottom thread in the bobbin is showing, you may find you need to loosen it a little. When everything is correct, you will see the loops forming as they fall off the flange at the back of the foot; they create quite a stunning effect. Try now to vary the length of the stitch so that some of the loops are close together and

35. The Buttercup Field *project completed.*

some are far apart. The width of the stitch can be varied but only slightly. Remember to finish with a straight stitch, otherwise the loops will flatten as you pull the material away from the machine.

Choose a coloured thread that matches one you have already used for hand loops. Meander over the hand loops in your embroidery with the machine loops. Do not be afraid to create some convoluted curves in the way you direct your machine. You will discover that such directions will enhance those you have already made, whereas straight lines would negate them.

Continue with as many different colours as you wish, following the same guidelines as before to help you decide how much of each colour to place in the various parts of your embroidery. For 90 per cent, match colour and tone and use a close stitch; for 10 per cent, open up the stitch length for different colours and tones. This machine stitch has the advantage of securing the hand loops, as well as adding sumptuous textures to the surface of the embroidery.

RECAPITULATION AND CONSOLIDATION

As before, it is useful to consolidate what we have achieved before engaging in something new. One of the aims of doing the projects in this book together is to learn how to deepen our understanding, and to broaden our knowledge of different methods and techniques. If you look back at Figs. 2 and 24, you will see that the methods and techniques we have used for The Buttercup Field are exactly the same as the embroideries depicting a wood of bluebells and a bough of may blossom. It is important to discover how many wonderful variations can be made in each technique. Take time to revise, renew and reinforce what you have started to understand.

Choose different subjects, make your pictures different sizes and select different colour schemes so that you may find new wonders in familiar methods.

Wonder is very much the affection of a philosopher; for there is no other beginning of philosophy than this.

Plato

The Honeysuckle and the Sweet-briar Rose: woodbine and eglantine

I know a bank where the wild thyme blows,
Where oxlips and the nodding violet grows.
Quite over-canopied with luscious woodbine
With sweet musk-roses and with eglantine.

William Shakespeare, *A Midsummer Night's Dream*

THE INSPIRATION

Few pleasures give more delight than summer hedgerows filled with honeysuckle and wild roses. Honeysuckle symbolizes affection, faithfulness and sweetness of disposition, and it has an especially sweet fragrance in the early evening. Its other name, 'woodbine', indicates another of its qualities, how it entwines other plants with its many tendrils. The wild rose poets call 'eglantine' is better known as sweet-briar or the rambler rose. Although the rose is generally considered to be a symbol of love, the eglantine is traditionally associated with pleasure mixed with pain.

Would you appoint some flower to reign
In matchless beauty on the plain,
The Rose (mankind will all agree)
The Rose, the Queen of Flowers should be.

Sappho

USING AND SELECTING THE SOURCES OF INSPIRATION

Although I have often seen these two plants entwining themselves around each other, I was unable to find them together this year. Because I particularly wanted to link them for our next project, I had to contrive a combined design from individual sources. Figs. 36 and 37 illustrate two such attempts, which set both plants against the wall on which the honeysuckle, the 'luscious woodbine', grows in my garden. I also included a few insects, a butterfly in one and a bumblebee in the other. However, there already seemed to be enough variety in the picture with the contrast of the two flowers, so I decided to omit the insects when it came to making the patterns from the designs.

You will see from Figs. 38 and 39 that I made two patterns from my two designs. You will surmise correctly that we will be making a pair of embroideries; we shall also be doing them concurrently.

Being engaged in a number of projects concurrently has many advantages. If we spend too long on any project without taking a rest, we

36 and 37. Preliminary drawings for The Honeysuckle and the Sweet-briar Rose *project.*

become tired and irritable; if we persist in continuing, we usually make mistakes. Therefore, it is better to stop and engage in another activity, not necessarily something completely different. Indeed, it could be one of our projects at a different stage. There is a psychological advantage in having a number of projects to work on concurrently. With other projects in reserve, we feel more able to take risks with the one we are engaged on at the moment. Most important of all, it allows the transference of our ideas to run more smoothly. We often think of different methods and techniques to try in each of our projects, but it is not possible to use all of them and we usually forget many of the ideas we think of. By having a number of projects which are being developed concurrently, we can put more of these ideas into practice. Thus this procedure encourages our creative spirit to be more free, our minds to grow more flexible and our skills to become more fluent.

Do please follow my designs and patterns for our next two projects or, if you wish, devise your own patterns from your own sources. Remember to keep the patterns clear and simple even if the design and your intended embroideries are to be complex.

Figs. 38 and 39 are simple line drawings, which will help us to position some very complicated shapes in very subtle tones and colours. If you found it helpful before to make several copies of the same pattern, then do so again. Figs. 40–43 emphasize different parts of the picture and indicate how to proceed at the collage stage of this project. Notice the importance of the direction of the lines denoting the stems. This was a deliberate exaggeration on my part in order to portray their convolutions.

Where blooms the woodbine faintly streaked
  with red,
And rests on every bough its tender head;
Round the young ash its turning branches meet,
Or crown the hawthorn with its odours sweet.

Robert Bloomfield

38. Above and below: master paper patterns for
The Honeysuckle and the Sweet-briar Rose *project.*

THE FABRIC COLLAGE STAGE

At the start of this chapter I mentioned that the two projects we shall be doing are both developments of what we learned in Chapter One. In Chapter Two, *The Buttercup Field* showed a different way of applying the collage, the same method in the first stage of machine embroidery, different hand embroidery techniques and a different final stage of machine embroidery. Although the procedure remained the same, the methods and techniques were varied and sometimes quite different. This project will also follow the same procedure — some of the methods and techniques will be slightly varied, others will be completely different. I suspect that you, like me, need familiar reference points to act as a firm foundation on which to base newfound knowledge.

Start by choosing some firm backing material. I chose reddish-brown hessian because I thought its colour would contribute very well to representing the area of wall. The dimensions of each piece of hessian were 560 × 480mm (22 × 19in). This allowed for the 'shrinking' process which embroidery causes, and for the edges of the material to be turned when the finished embroidery is stretched and framed. The final dimensions of both pieces are 460 × 350mm (18 × 14in), the same as the last project. However, whereas *The Buttercup Field* was a horizontal format, both of these are a vertical format. Sew round the edges of the hessian to prevent them from fraying, using a wide zigzag stitch on the sewing machine.

Now begin to choose your fabric scraps. Select varying types of material, as we have done before, and try to contrast different textures: rough with smooth and shiny with matt. Try also to contrast patterned with plain and transparent with opaque. In this way, you will be able to transform quite ordinary fabric into something amazingly pleasurable.

39. *Above and below: paper patterns, emphasizing areas representing the mass of leaves and wall.*

40. *Above and below: paper patterns, emphasizing areas representing the flowers and stems.*

Be guided by your original pictures to help your selection of colours. Glance now at my finished embroideries (Fig. 44) and you will see that the actual number of colours is limited to greens and pale browns, with a few pale reds ('pinks') and yellows. However, within this limited range I deliberately chose a large number of tones and hues. For example, for the area of the wall, which takes up the larger part of both embroideries, I chose a gold metallic fabric which is very pale yellow when it catches the light and grey rather than brown when it is in shadow. As well as a number of pale browns (beiges, buffs and fawns), I also included a few pale oranges, pale purples ('mauves'), pale reds ('pinks') and pale yellows because from a distance they blended with the other colours and seemed to take on the colour of the wall. This variety gives a scintillating effect to this area, which must not detract from the main subject of the flowers but at the same time must not be dull or drab. It should with all its subtle variations contribute to the entire harmony of the embroidery.

Variety is the condition of harmony.

J.F. Clarke

Take up the copy of each of your paper patterns which represents the area of the wall where the vertical stripes have been emphasized and the area depicting the mass of leaves is distinct from the wall (Figs. 40 and 41). Such an area is often referred to as 'background' but I try to avoid using this term because it carries with it connotations of not being very important. As a result it could be treated as not being of interest. At worst, particularly at the stage of drawing and designing on paper, it is deliberately forgotten and omitted altogether, with the remark, 'I'll do that later.' Those of you who have met me before, either on one of my courses or by reading one of my earlier books, will already know how important I consider it is to treat the composition as a whole entity right from the outset. Such a concept is crucial to those artists and craftspeople who are continually seeking for an integrated harmony in their work.

In a picture every part will be visible and will play the role conferred upon it, be it principal or secondary.

Henri Matisse

Cut from the paper patterns the areas which represent the mass of green leaves. Place these on the hessian backing material. These indicate where *not* to place the fabric pieces for the area representing the wall. Assemble together all the fabric pieces you have chosen for the wall. Cut them up into small, irregularly shaped pieces; some need not be much bigger than your thumbnail, others could be a little smaller. Cut some with straight edges and some with curved edges. Put them into individual heaps and arrange all your collage equipment on your working-hand side, just as we have done before. Stick these fabric pieces onto one piece of hessian backing, taking care not to run out of a heap of fabric which cannot be replenished. The two collages (and the two eventual embroideries) are intended to be considered as a pair. Although they will not be identical, there should be correlation between them and one such correlation is that whatever material is used in one is also used in the other.

Take into account the vertical stripe which is indicated on the pattern, but only by laying a straight side of any fabric you choose to place in a vertical direction in that position. Although this may seem to be inconsequential, it is, in fact, significant enough to infuse a sense of stability and alertness to the composition at this early stage. You may already be aware of how different directions of lines evoke different responses in us. Very generally speaking, all diagonals appear dynamic, mobile and exciting, whereas verticals and horizontals appear stable,

41 and 42. The completed stages of The Honeysuckle and the Sweet-briar Rose *project.*

still and quiet. Another reason for this implied vertical is that it will act as a foil and supporting contrast to the curves we shall be creating later on to form the flowers and stems. Now look at what you have achieved from a distance to check how you are progressing. If you need to change anything, for example because a tone or a colour is too strong a contrast, do so at once. Remember that transparent fabric is useful at this stage to blend in such contrasts.

Once you have completed this stage in one of the collages, complete this same stage in the other one. You have an excellent opportunity to put into practice the advantages of working on two or more pieces of work concurrently. You will discover that you can transfer ideas you think successful from one to the other immediately. Conversely, you may find that other things

you have done are neither suitable nor appropriate, in which case you should be able to remember, in this short space of time, not to repeat them! Thus the avoidance or transference of knowledge is more swiftly done by this method of concurrent work.

Now remove that part of the paper pattern which represents the mass of green leaves, and construct this area with the variety of green fabric you have chosen. When I constructed this area, I decided to keep the fabric pieces as various and undetermined as those representing the wall. I did not shape any of these pieces of fabric deliberately to look like leaves. My reason for this was that I wanted the illusion of a mass of leaves rather than an accumulation of individual ones, lest their potentially dominant shapes should detract from those of the flowers and stems, which were to be significant in the final composition. In order that neither of the areas representing the leaves or the wall should appear too solid, I also placed a few pale brown scraps of fabric in the area representing the leaves and a few green scraps of fabric occasionally around the perimeter of the green area, spilling over onto the area representing the wall. Try all this yourself in any way you think suitable. Check what you have done from a distance, and deal with any necessary amendments or additions before proceeding to the next stage.

Take up the other copies of your paper pattern (Figs. 42 and 43), which emphasize the flowers and the directions of the stems. Cut out the areas which represent the roses. Select a variety of fabrics in pale reds ('pinks') and some whites, and deal with each picture in turn. You may like to use the areas which you have just cut out as templates, so that you can form the petal shapes and the shapes within each petal exactly. You will remember that we used this method of working in our first project, *Primroses*. Alternatively, you may like to continue working 'freehand' by cutting up small pieces of fabric in a random way and forming the roses with these composite pieces, like a mosaic. I preferred to use the first method and constantly referred to my original drawings and paintings. But, as this is your third project, I urge you to make some of these decisions for yourself. Trust in your instinct.

Continue to construct the rose and honeysuckle flowers in the method you prefer, and with the shapes, tones and colours you deem appropriate, until they begin to take on the form of the flowers and also make a balanced harmony in the picture. Do not be afraid to use again some of the colours you have already used to represent the wall, for example, pale yellow and pale red ('pink'). Do not worry if they seem to disappear into the 'background'; there are some new methods and techniques later on in this project which will counteract any such effect. If we want to achieve a balanced har-

mony in our compositions, it is very important to repeat elements such as these. It is not necessary to overstate everything; it often helps the picture to merge and blend, with deliberate understatement. Indeed, let us try this again with the flowing stems!

Cut out some very thin, short strips of green and pale brown fabric from some of the left-over pieces used to represent the wall and the leaves. Using the lines denoting the stems in the paper pattern to guide you, stick these strips in broken lines to suggest the direction of the stems. Deliberately emphasize some by placing a green strip or two over an area representing part of the wall, and by placing some strips of 'wall' fabric over the green 'leaves' fabric.

Now reverse the process so that you merely suggest the direction of the stems by deliberate understatement, placing pale brown on pale brown and green on green. Check from a distance to see how both collages are progressing. Take advantage of this concurrent method of working to avoid repeating something which is inappropriate or to transfer something which is successful.

The Rose

Thou blushing Rose, within whose virgin leaves,
The wanton wind to sport himself presumes,
Whilst from their rifled wardrobe he receives
For his wings purple, for his breath perfumes:
Blown in the morning, thou shalt fade e'er noon;
What boots a life which in such haste forsakes
   thee!
Thou'rt wondrous frolic, being to die so soon
And passing proud a little colour makes thee.

Sir Richard Fanshawe

TIME TO PAUSE FOR RESTFUL THOUGHT

Once more the time has come for us to have a rest from our practical work. We have put into practice the precept 'A change is as good as a rest' by changing our attention from one piece of work to another, but it is wise to have another kind of change by leaving them altogether for a while. Let us look at three pieces of work by other embroiderers who were also inspired by the season of summer.

Fig. 45 shows part of a necklace by Heide Jenkins. The honeycomb arrangement is made in two layers by a linked framework of hexagon frames cut from stiff plastic and closely wrapped with silk thread. My reason for including this delicately worked piece is not only its obvious association with bees, and thus flowers, but also because of its finely subdued colouring, delicately contrasted textures and clearly delineated forms. We have just been concerned in our own project with the balance between emphasis and understatement. Here is a very fine example of how the exactly delineated forms of the hexagon frames of the honeysuckle and the curving contours of the bees are counterbalanced by the similar-toned, subdued colouring. This subdued colouring is enriched by, and acts as a foil to, the fine detailing of the centres of the hexagons and the wings of the bees, worked in gold thread.

And, as it works, the industrious bee
Computes its time as well as we.
How could such sweet and wholesome hours
Be reckoned but with herbs and flowers!

Andrew Marvell, *The Garden*

The embroidery illustrated in Fig. 46 is by Jean Muchelec and is derived from an image on a greetings card. She started it on one of my fabric collage and machine embroidery courses and finished it at home. I am pleased to include it here because it is an excellent example of how it is possible to make a fine and intricate embroidery from a simple starting point. It is also a good example of how the contrast of certain elements can invigorate the life of the picture. For example, the blue tits and the honeysuckle flowers and leaves are emphasized by the darkness of

43. Honeycomb Necklace *(detail) by Heide Jenkins, early 1980s. Fabric construction and embroidery. Photograph by Heide Jenkins.*

the surrounding brown areas. Furthermore, the technique used for the honeysuckle is different from that used for the blue tits. Sometimes if too many differences are present in a picture the effect can be distracting, but fortunately this is not so here because of the element of repetition. Whereas contrast gives life to the picture, repetition of similarities helps to bind and link all the elements of the composition together. Here both techniques are repeated and contrasted throughout the embroidery, which contributes to the balanced harmony of the entire composition.

Contrast increases the splendour of beauty, but it disturbs its influence; it adds to its attractiveness, but diminishes its power.

John Ruskin

Such balances between contrast and repetition, and between emphasis and understatement, are exquisitely present in *Wild Roses* (Fig. 47) by Helena Baily, who used one of my drawings in coloured pencils as her starting point. The consistent vertical direction is the evident linking factor, and it also gives a bright and alert character to the picture. To contrast such a repetition

44. Blue Tits and Honeysuckle *by Jean Muchelec,*
1992. Fabric collage with machine and hand
embroidery.

of direction, a strong difference of tone and a pairing of complementary colours has been employed. If you examine the picture carefully, you will see how a pale red and an orange-yellow thread has been included in the green and blue area representing the leaves, and how a blue thread is present in the darker tones of the flowers near the orange-yellow centres. Helena Baily herself is very conscious of such things, and her approach is a valuable lesson for all of us:

> It is interesting to create a flowing design of rich colours within the discipline of the vertical stitch of varying lengths. This was inspired by the vertical inclination of the warp in woven tapestry which disciplines the variety of colour in the design. I began by constructing the basic shapes in their main colours, taking care to leave space for the addition of complementary colours. It is extraordinary how even one or two stitches in complementary colours bring life into the main shapes. This is not a technique for those who want to finish a piece of work quickly. The fascination lies in the leisurely in-and-out motion of the needle (and its little sound!) and the thoughtful contemplation of its colourful design.

THE FIRST MACHINE EMBROIDERY STAGE

Filled with renewed enthusiasm, let us return to our project with 'thoughtful contemplation'. This stage uses two different techniques. The first technique is one you have practised before; the second technique will be new to you.

First of all position your heart, mind and body in a comfortable and attentive attitude by practising the 'Golden Cord' exercise (see page 6) or

45. Wild Roses *by Helena Baily, 1993. Vertical*
straight stitching with Danish cotton thread
on slub silk.

by any other means which you prefer. Then prepare all the equipment you need for the same kind of free embroidery as we have been practising with all our previous projects. Set up your sewing machine, attach a darning foot, insert a thick needle and lower or cover the 'feed' according to your instruction manual. The stitch length needs to be set at zero, and the stitch width at the widest zigzag. You will also need a variety of threads which correspond to the coloured fabrics you used in the collage stage.

Start sewing your collage pieces onto the backing material in exactly the same way as you have done before. Use the same guide to help you measure the proportions: for most of the picture match both colour and tone, but for very small areas you can mismatch both colour and tone. In this way, all the threads contribute to the balanced harmony of the picture rather than being used only in isolated sections. Remember to do any such mismatchings in very small amounts, otherwise they may turn into unsightly intrusions rather than harmonious contributions. Once you have finished using each thread in one picture, start sewing with them in the other so that both your embroideries develop concurrently.

When all your fabric pieces have been sewn with at least three or four stitches in each picture, assess your progress by looking at them from a distance so that you can see how they are developing. If, by instinct, you feel that more stitching is needed, either with different threads or ones you have already used, then do so immediately.

When you feel that this stage is complete, as our other earlier projects were 'complete' at this stage, we can proceed to a new technique. We have already made deliberate attempts to understate some features, such as flowers, leaves and stems, by matching similar colours and tones at the collage stage, even to the extent where some features seemed to disappear into other parts of the picture. We are now going to give some emphasis to these features.

Clip the presser foot onto your sewing machine and raise or uncover the 'feed' because the stitch length is to be operative. It is possible to alter the length and width of the stitch during this process; indeed it is *necessary* to do so in order to give variety to the design. However, the stitch length should vary only slightly; sometimes try using it as close as possible so that a satin stitch is achieved, at other times open out the length a little to achieve lines of stitching which are not quite as dense. The stitch width can be as wide or narrow as you like, according to the requirements of the design.

Set up your sewing machine with a coloured thread which matches one of the fabric pieces you have used to construct the honeysuckle. Remember to put a *cotton* thread of the same colour in the bottom. Set the stitch length to be quite close and the stitch width to zero, so that the resulting stitch will be straight and quite close in length.

Place one of your embroideries in the machine so that the needle is positioned just above the centre of one of the honeysuckle flowers. The aim is to sew around each of the tapering pieces of fabric (each represents a honeysuckle floret) in turn. The straight stitch matches the width of the narrowest part of each piece of fabric; as you sew, increase the width of the stitch gradually as the fabric widens. Try to ensure that the needle penetrates the fabric piece for each alternate stitch, and falls just outside its outer edge for the next stitch. Your stitching will thus apply the fabric neatly to the backing material, and will also provide a certain amount of emphasis according to how you match or mismatch the colour and tone of the thread you use. If you match colours and tones, you will achieve a blending effect; if you mismatch colours and tones, the result will be a contrasting effect. As you travel around each piece of fabric, continue to widen or narrow the stitch width as you think appropriate. If you wish to make the stitch width a little more dense or farther apart, then do so. As you move towards the tapering end of the honeysuckle floret, taper the width of the stitch in order to finish, as you started, with a straight stitch. Continue stitching with this thread in other parts of the picture which are of the same colour and tone for most of the time, but occasionally sew around some of the fabric pieces with another colour of the same tone. For example, if you are using pale yellow thread, you could occasionally sew around some pale red fabric. It is not always necessary to sew around the whole piece of material with the same thread; you could sew part of the edge and then continue with another coloured thread later on. In this way you can vary the colours and tones of your stitching in very subtle ways.

Once you have finished taking a particular thread through one of your pictures, proceed to use it in the same way with the other picture. Use this concurrent way of working to help transfer methods which are successful and to avoid repeating any mistakes you have made. Change and vary your threads in colours, tones and textures, and alter the length and width of your stitch as you feel appropriate. If it helps you to follow my earlier guidelines on how to match tones and colours for most of the picture, but also to mismatch them occasionally, then continue to do so. However, if other ideas occur to you, then follow those. Most of us find that a few rules help us, but we need to follow our instinct as well!

A few strong instincts and a few plain rules.

William Wordsworth

THE HAND EMBROIDERY STAGE

Once you have completed this first stage of machine embroidery, you are ready to embellish your picture with hand stitching. The embroidery stitches I employed in Fig. 44 may not be easily discernible. Although I wanted to enrich the surface, I did not want my stitches to be an intrusive element; rather I wanted them to enhance and unify what was already there. I covered the area representing the wall and leaves with tiny seed stitches in various yarns and threads of matching tones and colours. Also in matching tones and colours, I couched down lines of the same yarns and threads around some of the edges of the pieces of fabric and the lines of machine stitching which represent the flowers and stems. Do as little or as much of this kind of enrichment as you like. I try to achieve a surface which is really sumptuous, but the resulting effect should not be garish or brash. Therefore I make a number of understatements by blending and merging colours, tones and textures. You may prefer to exercise a little more restraint, or even to be more extreme! Whatever we choose to do, let us all follow Helena Baily's example by listening ιo the needle's 'little sound'. By using our senses in this way, we may focus fully on the sensitive process which in turn enables our final embroideries to be that much more sensitive. I have to admit that this stage took twice as long as the first two stages and I enjoyed every moment. I hope you do too!

Let us start a new religion with one commandment, enjoy thyself.

Israel Zangwill

THE SECOND MACHINE EMBROIDERY STAGE AND CONCLUSION OF THE PROJECT

You may discover that within the profusion of seed stitches and the amount of couched lines, some appear too prominent. Rather than unpicking them, you could try, as I did, to subdue them slightly by machining over them, using the following two couching methods. The first method I used was to return to our now well-practised form of free embroidery with a darning foot. Using a variety of stitch widths, I machined over all the hand-couched lines and seed stitches which appeared too proud and pronounced. The second method I used was to cover much of the surface with one of the set patterns some sewing machines have. My sewing machine has a set pattern which forms a delicately shaped star. I fed this into one of the machine's 'memories', together with some straight stitches so that the star pattern did not repeat itself too often and appear relentless. I attached the presser foot and raised the 'feed', which is the procedure for achieving such set patterns. I then embellished the surface of the embroideries with this pattern, taking care to match tone and colour nearly all the time because of the very real danger that the star pattern might invade intrusively rather than enhance. A sure way to gauge this is that each stitch should be detected only at close quarters and not from a distance. If you have such pattern-making devices on your machine, try one in this way. You should find the method intriguing to practise and entrancing to behold!

Fig. 44 shows the completed stages of this project, which include beads sewn over the embroidered surfaces. Many years ago I bought a jar of very small antique beads in a street market; they are mainly dark brown and grey, and had been waiting to be used for far too long! I risked placing a few in similar-toned and -coloured areas in the embroidery. As long as I could not see them from even a short distance, I felt that I could continue in this manner throughout both embroideries and in the end I found that I had sewn on a couple of thousand! The flowers also required a similar treatment, so they were arrayed with a few hundred palest of pale red and clear glass beads. This is another way to help create the unity of your composition by being both splendid yet quietly understated.

Unity, agreement, is always silent or soft-voiced;
it is only discord that loudly proclaims itself.

Thomas Carlyle

I hope you have enjoyed the projects in this 'Summer' chapter. Do remember that it is by regular and constant practice that we develop our skills. Although we are halfway through the seasons, we have really only just started on this journey which can extend far beyond the final pages of this book. I mention this because fears and uncertainties about our abilities often trouble our creative processes. If this is happening to you, cast such cares aside and focus on the pleasurable but uncertain learning process. As William Congreve said, 'Uncertainty and expectation are the joys of life.'

46. (Above) Daisies and Cornflowers. Watercolour, 1989.

47. (Right) Daisies and Cornflowers. Embroidery, 1989.

CHAPTER THREE

Autumn

*Thou crownest the year with thy goodness:
and they clouds drop fatness.*

*They shall drop upon the pastures of the
wilderness: and the little hills shall rejoice on
every side.*

*The folds shall be full of sheep: the valleys also
shall stand so thick with corn, that they shall
laugh and sing.*

Psalm 65

This lovely passage from the Psalms encapsulates the abundance of riches which autumn harvests promise us. It is a passage full of gladness and thankfulness; autumn is the consummation of the growth of summer which was anticipated in spring. I particularly like the reference to the laughing and singing valleys! However, autumn is also often thought of as a melancholy season, which draws our minds to thoughts of mortality and the fleeting nature of our delights and joys.

Although autumn seems to possess this curiously ambivalent nature, we shall concentrate for all our projects in this chapter only on those aspects which are joyful, exuberant and full of gladness. Do not imagine that I am unaware of the sad, the difficult and the seemingly impossible facets of human existence; moreover, I applaud those artists and craftspeople who manifest a melancholy nature in their work.

*48. The River by Verina Warren, 1980s. Mixed
embroidery and painting techniques. Photograph by
Verina Warren.*

However, my desire is to enable us to cope with such issues by focusing on happier things which, indeed, are just as real.

We shall look at squirrels at work and foxes at rest, at mossy stones and glistening sphagnum pools, at silver birches set ablaze by the setting sun and spiders' webs among the brambles, only just discernible through mists and dew. We shall also see how the cornfields have turned from summer greens to autumnal browns of subtle tints and mellow hues.

Most of the methods and techniques that we shall employ in this chapter will be variations of those we have tried before. However, the first project is very different from any we have explored so far. It is a method I call 'drawing with the needle'. Let us now try it!

Season of mists and mellow fruitfulness!
Close bosom-friend of the maturing sun;
Conspiring with him how to load and bless
With fruit the vines that round the thatch-eaves
*   run;*
To blend with apples the moss'd cottage-trees,
And fill all fruit with ripeness to the core;
To swell the gourd, and plump the hazel shells
With a sweet kernel; to set budding more,
And still more, later flowers for the bees,
Until they think warm days will never cease,
For Summer has o'er-brimm'd their clammy cells.

John Keats, *To Autumn*

The Silver Birches

THE INSPIRATION

'The lady of the woods', as Coleridge described the birch, is surely one of the most graceful trees in our countryside. It was held sacred by Neolithic man and in the Middle Ages its sap was thought to possess medicinal qualities. I am fortunate enough to have two tall, slender silver birch trees growing in my garden, which give excellent shelter to the early primroses and bluebells. Nevertheless, I have chosen a watercolour by Sutton Palmer to act as the starting point and guide for our next project. I had always wanted to make a free translation of this illustration from one of my natural history books; I also thought it was about time I put into practice my oft-repeated suggestion that you use other people's work. It is important to make a free translation and not an exact copy, otherwise we will be in danger of infringing the laws of copyright (see page 12). Use my free translation if you wish, or a picture from your own supply.

Fall, leaves, fall; die flowers, away;
Lengthen night and shorten day;
Every leaf speaks bliss to me
Fluttering from the Autumn tree.

Emily Brontë, *Song*

PREPARATION AND DEVELOPING THE SOURCE OF INSPIRATION

The method we shall be using for this project is just free machine embroidery. We shall be 'drawing' with the needle. Imagine that the needle is your pen and the different coloured threads are the various inks.

Fig. 49 is my freehand drawing, an adapted version of the watercolour illustration by Sutton Palmer. If the idea of drawing brings you out in a rash, never fear! For the time being, you can trace my picture to establish the main contours as your guidelines, and then shade in the various tones freehand. Try it and see how you get on; you will never know what you might be capable of unless you try. It is helpful to engage in a number of these kinds of intermediate stages because they help us to get to know the composition of the subject better and to make any changes that we find necessary.

Another important stage is to draw your

49. The Silver Birches *pencil drawing.*

composition directly on the fabric. So that I could see what I was doing as clearly as possible, I used white cotton as the backing fabric and drew with coloured pencils. You can detect some of these coloured guidelines in Fig. 50, which is a detail of the embroidery in its early stages. Although you could use fabric paints, I have found that the pencil line is more closely related to the line created by the sewing machine. Before you draw on the backing fabric, it helps if you put it in an embroidery hoop or frame first.

Because we shall be engaged in a lot of embroidery which will cover the entire surface of the fabric, it is necessary to attach the fabric to some kind of frame. I stapled my backing fabric to a home-made embroidery frame cut from ply-wood, whose inner dimensions were about 220

× 225mm (9 × 10in). This is larger than any I know to be available commercially and it is still possible to embroider right into the centre of the fabric. You can easily get one made for you by asking a friendly wood merchant to cut it with a jig-saw. Remember to ask him to round the inner, and especially the outer, corners. This will help its manoeuvrability in the sewing machine.

As this is your first time with this method, my suggestion is that you keep the dimensions of the whole picture well within the inner dimensions of the frame so that you start and finish your embroidery without having to shift the fabric. However, I wanted my embroidery to be taller than my frame allowed in order to depict the gracefulness of the trees and to include a lot of bracken at the bottom of the picture. I therefore had to embroider my picture in two stages. If you are feeling adventurous, you could do the same.

STARTING AND COMPLETING THE PROJECT: DRAWING WITH THE NEEDLE

If you have not done so already, start by practising the 'Golden Cord' exercise (see page 6) so that you are in a calm but attentive state of mind. Set up your sewing machine with the 'feed' lowered or covered, according to your instruction manual. Put both stitch length and stitch width to zero because we want to make a straight stitch. We could dispense with the darning foot altogether and sew with a bare needle, because the backing fabric is now stretched in a frame. However, I have found that at the early stages of this method some stitches are missed, so I prefer to continue using the darning foot.

Fig. 50 shows a detail of the early stages of this embroidery. You will notice that several colours have already been used and that they have all been taken through that part of the picture as a whole. Although it is done entirely with a 'straight' stitch, it is possible to achieve any direction required according to how you move the fabric. Thus I was able to create long,

50. The early stages of The Silver Birches *project.*

flowing directions for the trunks and branches of the trees and small circular directions for the leaves. If you now look at the finished embroidery (Fig. 51), you will notice shorter and straighter directions to depict the movement of the bracken.

Try this method yourself. Thread the machine with any colour you think is suitable. Match the colour with a *cotton* thread in the bobbin and start sewing. Move the fabric in the directions given to you by the coloured drawing on the fabric. Once you have taken one colour through, continue with another, and another. Glance again at Fig. 50 and you will see that quite a lot has been started with just one green, one orange, one yellow and one brown thread.

Although the design is drawn on the fabric, it is as well to keep the original source close by. I

had mine near me all the time; I even turned it round when it was necessary to turn the frame as I was sewing.

The rest of the picture (Fig. 51) follows the same procedure. Try using several hues and tones of the same colour and also try using metallic thread. I contrasted a gold thread in the leaves with a silver thread in the trunks; the fact that they are both glittering threads created a linking factor by means of repetition.

Those of you who, like me, are attempting to embroider a picture larger than the frame will have to complete the first part and then shift the fabric along the frame. This means re-stapling the remainder of the fabric in position. It will also be necessary to keep (preferably in order)

51. The Silver Birches *project completed.*

all the threads which were used in the first part, so that you can use them again. This will preserve the continuity and unanimity of the composition.

THE CONTINUED VALUE OF CONCURRENT WORK

The very first illustration in this book, *Sunrise* (Fig. 1), is embroidered by this method of 'drawing' with the needle. The very last illustration, *Sunset* (Fig. 74), is also embroidered in this technique. Because I had planned that these three embroideries should be stitched in this particular method, it seemed necessary that I should work on them concurrently. We have discussed the virtues of this practice but I cannot express enough times how useful it is. There often comes a point in our work when we are not sure of what to do or where to go. It is at this point that it is useful to direct our attention to another embroidery. It is easier to transfer an idea about technique, procedure or interpretation from one embroidery to another than if we had started and completed one on its own.

Try a few more embroideries in this technique. Choose any subject you like; this method will suit almost anything as long as the details are not too intricate. You will find that there are many ways of directing the fabric which will, in turn, cause a large number of stitch variations. Some have specific names. When the stitch forms small curves without overlapping, it is known as 'vermicelli stitch'. If the stitch forms small circles which overlap each other, it is known as 'granite stitch'. In fact, Fig. 1 is completely embroidered in granite stitch.

The Badger (Fig. 52) is embroidered in granite stitch and has a fine variety of stitch direction. The embroiderer is Daphne Ashby and it was she who first gave me the idea of stitching pictures specifically in this way. I am delighted to include this example of her work, which she embroidered especially for this book; it is now owned by the Wirral and Cheshire Badger Group.

52. The Badger *by Daphne Ashby, 1993. Free machine embroidery.*

TIME TO PAUSE FOR RESTFUL THOUGHT

I want us to continue looking at Daphne Ashby's embroidery of the badger, from which we may learn a great deal. It is sad that the badger's only enemy is mankind. Even though today this slow-moving nocturnal creature is lawfully protected, there is still much prejudice against it. I

53. The Flowerpot, *detail from* A Walk in Assisi *by Audrey Walker, 1992. Hand embroidery. Photograph by Audrey Walker.*

hope by including the 'brock' or 'bawson', as the badger is sometimes known, our sensibilities will be heightened for this and the rest of the animal kingdom likewise persecuted.

Daphne Ashby's depiction of the badger is very late in the autumn when the first flurry of a November snow has sprinkled the ground. Although quite numerous, the badger is seldom seen and his tracks are often the only indication of his presence. Here, however, we see him emerging from his set, perhaps to replace his soiled bedding with fresh dry bracken or crisp autumn leaves; badgers are known to be scrupulously clean! Notice how the white and grey threads are used to depict both the badger and the snow. Grey threads have also been used to construct the upper part of the composition. Not only does this treatment effectively represent the animal's natural camouflage, it helps to unify the picture. You will remember that repetition is an important constituent of harmony. Notice how the brown and the yellow threads are distributed in different parts of the composition so that they balance each other. The whole picture seems to emanate a stillness upon which it is extremely pleasant to meditate.

Fig. 53 by Audrey Walker shows a flowerpot full of rich autumn-coloured flowers. We have already looked at two of her pieces and learned much from them. I have chosen this particular detail from a much larger work because it shows how well it stands up to close examination. I have always believed that embroideries, paintings, drawings and in fact all works of art should be able to withstand such scrutiny as well as being seen to work from a distance. Barbara Hepworth said, 'It is the finishing touches that make a work of art truly great.' This detail is an excellent example of how the very fine stitch directions give both a unity and a quietly throbbing energy to the picture. It is as if the plants have been softly caressed by a sudden breeze. Notice also how this finely detailed stitching gives as much importance to the flowerpot and the ground, with its subtle tracery of shadows, as

to the flowers and leaves. You will remember we discussed the importance of the background during *The Honeysuckle and the Sweet-briar Rose* project. You will also remember how we discussed the importance of stitch direction in the work of Eirian Short and Verina Warren.

Now we will turn back to another delightful embroidery by Verina Warren (Fig. 48), which opens this chapter. Once again, we can learn much from her example. In this celebration of early autumn, we hardly notice the poppies in amongst the sun-bleached grasses and yellow ragwort. In Fig. 32, *Poppy Field*, we saw how the poppies seemed to emanate a glowing vibration. This was because the red of the poppies were juxtaposed with the green of the unripened corn. You will remember that if you want to enhance a colour, you can do so by placing it near its complementary. As red is complementary to green, this is how the glowing vibration was achieved. Contrast of tone is also helpful. In the same picture, particularly on the righthand side, the mid-toned red poppies are enhanced by the pale-toned green corn. You will also recall that, in order to achieve a blending effect where contrast is not required, you can match similar colours and tones. In *Poppy Field* the poppies seem to merge with the green corn rather than appearing dominant; this is because the red of the poppies and the green of the corn are of the same tone.

Now let us return to Verina Warren's autumn picture (Fig. 48), with its majestic river gliding slowly through spacious meads. Here the reds of the poppies seem not to be quite so pronounced because in most of the picture they are positioned either next to similar-toned greens or near the orange-yellow hues of the sun-bleached grasses and ragwort flowers. The reason the river is so noticeable is because its blueness is not far from the orange-yellow of the areas we have just examined. In order to prevent the river being *too* noticeable, its blue-green colour is repeated in the sky; green colours, which are close to blue, have been placed in the forms of the grasses, shrubs and trees near the river so that a *progression* occurs. In very subtle ways, the entire picture has been constructed to balance the effect of contrast with the effect of blending, where neither is too violent nor too diffuse. As with all of Verina Warren's work, the embroidery which constructs the central panel is enhanced by the different technique of the outer part of the picture, which is painted. Notice also how the various directions of both brushmark and stitch complement and resolve themselves variously to form a complete whole.

Everything I see in the fields is to me an object, and I can look at the same rivulet, or at a handsome tree, every day of my life, with new pleasure. This indeed is partly the effect of a natural taste for rural beauty, and partly the effect of habit; for I never in all my life have let slip the opportunity of breathing fresh air, and of conversing with Nature, when I could fairly catch it.

William Cowper

The Blackberries and the Spider's Web in the Hedgerow

Come, let us go into the lane, love mine,
And mark and gather what the Autumn grows:
The creamy elder mellowed into wine,
The russet hip that was the pink-white rose;
The amber woodbine into rubies turned,
The blackberry that was the bramble born

Alfred Austin, *An Answer*

THE INSPIRATION

Sometimes I am asked whether I draw inspiration from the fabric. The answer is, of course, that I am always being guided by the nature of the fabrics and materials I use. Their various colours, tones and textures are a continuing influence throughout the whole of the embroidery's progress, from the beginning to the very end. I am equally guided by the nature of the threads I use. The different qualities of machine and hand embroidery cottons, silks and synthetic threads all have a role to play. Inspiration also comes from the nature of the subject itself, and this has been the mainspring of all the projects in this book. Sometimes the first gleam of an idea comes from poetry, or even music. We do, after all, possess five senses so why not allow the sense of hearing as well as sight and touch to contribute to our projects?

Several influences prompted this project. First, there were the blackberries themselves. I have childhood memories of blackberry-picking, and the subsequent treats of pies and jellies. When I used to teach full-time, before I went freelance, the blackberries always ripened at the beginning of the autumn term so I never had a chance to draw or paint them. The very first series of drawings I made when I resigned my full-time job was of blackberries. Since then, every September I make an effort to try and draw them.

The other subject of this project is the spider's web, which is particularly noticeable in autumn when it can be seen sparkling with dewdrops in the early morning. I have on my bookshelves an anthology of poems about the countryside illustrated by Gordon Beningfield. There is one sketch of a spider's web in amongst the brambles which I find very evocative of autumn, and both the sketch and the poems have contributed to this project.

As for the fabrics, threads and particularly the beads, each have beckoned me to their qualities as if to say 'Use me sometimes for berries' or

'We'd be very effective as rain or dewdrops'! Although many sources may contribute to the project, the visual source should be uppermost, otherwise there is a very real danger of producing stereotypes. Even though we may *think* we have all the information in our heads, few of us can store in memory all those subtle nuances and details of tone and colour. Therefore, let us keep our visual sources close by us throughout the making of the entire project, so that they may continue to inspire us at all stages. Remember also that these sources are for us to use as guides. If we copy them slavishly, we will negate the possibility of responding to the other sources which inspire us, such as the fabrics and the threads.

> *Never forget the material you are working with and try always to use it for what it can do best: if you feel yourself hampered with the material in which you are working, instead of being helped by it, you have so far not learned your business. The special limitations of the material should be a pleasure to you, not a hindrance.*

William Morris, *Textiles*

STARTING AND COMPLETING THE FABRIC COLLAGE STAGE

By now you will be familiar with how to prepare a paper pattern from your various sources (see page 15). Just remember that the pattern is for your use and guidance in the early stages of the project. If you wish to proceed without a pattern, allowing the picture to emerge gradually, then please do so. It will mean taking a lot of risks and probably making a lot of mistakes as well. You will also meet some unexpected surprises of a positive nature which might not have happened by other means. Why not live a little

54. The Blackberries and the Spider's Web in the Hedgerow completed. Photograph by Brian Nevitt.

dangerously sometimes? To encourage you to take this stimulating plunge, I too am approaching this project without a clear plan, allowing the picture to develop as it wants to.

Begin by placing all the visual material near you: all your pictures of brambles and, perhaps, other hedgerow plants, together with those of spiders' webs. You never know when it will be necessary to refer to some detail or other.

Assemble a range of dark and mid-toned brown and green fabrics of as many different kinds as possible, in a wide variety of textures. It is important not to have many, if any, pale tones for the green and brown areas of the hedgerow, otherwise neither the bramble flowers and berries nor the spider's web might be seen. However, it is equally important that these details are not too obviously prominent. You will remember that we discussed this while we were working on *The Honeysuckle and the Sweet-briar Rose* project.

I discovered that discreet use of glittering and metallic fabrics of mainly dark tones, placed in areas which represent shadows and recesses, is unexpectedly effective. The sudden gleam and sparkle caused by the reflection of light on such fabrics are akin to the half-light sometimes perceived in dense undergrowth and hedgerows. Such light will link and merge with the highlights on the berries and the dewdrops on the spider's web. Although these details need to manifest themselves, they must not do so excessively, otherwise the embroidery might look obviously brash and crude. The intention is that the blackberries and the spider's web should be only just discernible through the autumn mists and dew. The sumptuous richness of the embroidery's surface should be subtly stated!

Sew round the edges of the hessian to prevent them fraying, using a wide zigzag stitch on the sewing machine. Place small pieces of brown and green fabric on the hessian background (which can be either brown or green). Choose the size for your finished picture, remembering to leave an ample margin to allow for 'shrinking'

during the embroidery process, and also so that it can be turned under when the final piece of work is stretched. My completed embroidery (Fig. 54) is 460 × 350mm (18 × 14in), but you could make yours larger or smaller, just as you wish. Cut the fabric pieces at random or precisely, or both, as we have practised before in our other projects (see page 40). Be guided by your visual source material in how you assemble these pieces. Be also guided by your own innate sense of design and balance. Allow every stage of this project to grow harmoniously, and to be harmonious at the completion of each stage. Attach these fabric pieces with glue, as we did before (see page 40).

Now choose fabrics in pale reds ('pinks'), dark reds, purples, dark blues and black. These will represent the bramble flowers and berries. Cut out very small shapes and use both your visual source material and your instinct to assemble these pieces in the most balanced and harmonious way, as you did before. If you wish to include other plants in your picture, then do so. I so liked how 'The amber woodbine into rubies turned' in Alfred Austin's poem that I decided to include some dark red berries, which happily linked and matched with the unripe berries of the bramble.

The spider's web and the dewdrops are not included at this stage. Indeed, they are not dealt with until much later, after the machine embroidery stage. This means that the picture is not constructed holistically, as in all our other projects; there all the features and elements of the picture were stated, if only in part, in the early stages. This 'piecemeal' approach is a risk but there is a feeling of fearful joy about working in this way.

THE MACHINE EMBROIDERY STAGE

Begin by sewing all the small fabric pieces onto the hessian background in the same way as we have done before (see page 25). Remember to clip on the darning foot, lower or cover the 'feed', insert a thick needle (size about 90 or 100), set the stitch length to zero and, as before, set the stitch width to the widest zigzag for the early part of this stage. The darning foot is to facilitate free embroidery without having to use a frame or hoop, and the purpose of starting with the widest zigzag stitch is so that the fabric pieces are more quickly and efficiently sewn to the hessian background.

When all the fabric pieces are securely attached to the hessian background, experiment with developing certain areas of your picture with more concentrated stitches. Choose the areas and the coloured threads which you think appropriate. There were several areas which called my attention: one area was that which formed the berries. In order to create more definition than was possible by the collage method, I needed to embellish them with a range of pale- to dark-toned colours, depending on whether they represented ripe or unripe berries. I did this with granite stitch, which we discussed in our previous project (see page 72). I set the stitch width to zero and moved the fabric in very small circular movements until the forms became delineated.

Another area of my picture which needed attention was the leaves, in particular their 'toothed' edges. I attempted to create this effect by bringing up the 'feed', putting on the presser foot and programming the sewing machine to make one of its set patterns: two tiny pointed leaves. By moving the fabric slightly irregularly, it was possible to achieve a toothed effect around the edges of the leaves. A further area which required definition was the bramble flowers. Although each petal had been cut individually from pale red fabric of various kinds, it was still necessary to clarify the edges by sewing round each petal with variously tapered zigzag stitches.

The final area which needed embellishment was that composed of all the mid-toned and dark brown fabric. Because all the other parts of the picture had been given further attention,

these areas, by comparison, looked somewhat neglected. I chose another set pattern on my sewing machine, one which creates a tiny flower. I carefully matched the tone of the brown thread with the tone of the brown fabric so that none of these stitches were noticeable except at very close distance. Understatement was paramount. When you are developing areas of your picture, try to balance definition with understatement.

TIME TO PAUSE FOR RESTFUL THOUGHT

Before we proceed to the final part of our project, let us pause and reflect upon four other textile pictures which possess certain qualities that will assist our progress in this and all our subsequent embroideries.

Liquid Amber (Fig. 55) depicts a pile of fallen leaves. It was started by Doreen Hooper on one of my courses and she was kind enough to complete it at home especially for this book. It is an excellent example of how contrasting elements like colour, tone and texture can enliven a composition.

All the colours in the picture are either primary or secondary; no actual browns have been used, which partly accounts for its lively quality. This is enhanced by the minor, but important, inclusion of green near the red, the pale-toned yellows juxtaposed near dark-toned reds and greens, and the inclusion of sparkling fabrics such as sequins and sequin waste in conjunction with matt fabrics and threads. Variously directed stitches also contribute to the liveliness of the composition.

Whether ye wave above the early flow'rs
In lively green; or whether, rustling sere,
Ye fly on playful winds, around my feet,
In dying Autumn; lovely are your bow'rs,
Ye early-dying children of the year;
Holy the silence of your calm retreat.

William Barnes, *Leaves*

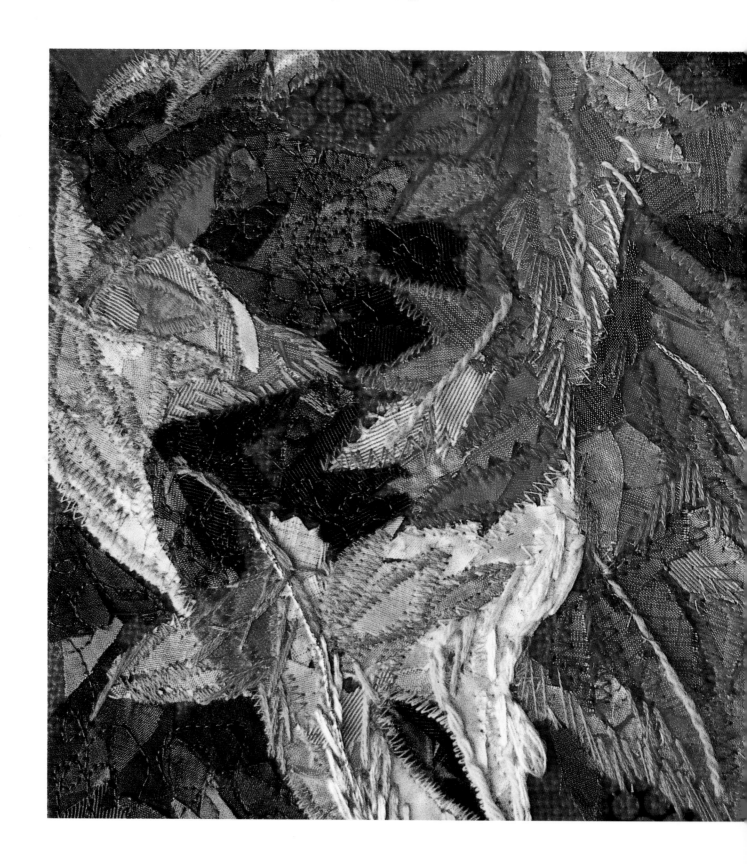

56. Bark II *(detail) by Josie Durham, 1992. Felt construction. Photograph by Josie Durham.*

Bark II (Fig. 56) is a detail of one of a pair of felt panels by Josie Durham. I have chosen it particularly for the range of colours she has perceived in the bark of a yew tree. A rich and plentiful supply of source material, in the form of her own sketches, photographs and large-scale pastel drawings, guided her throughout the process. She describes her work below:

I was particularly excited by the way the bark split and cracked, creating fissures, interlocking shapes and cast shadows. It was also fascinating to see the great variety of colours in the bark, which ranged through greys, lilacs, beiges, russets, browns, olive greens, shadowy blacks and many others besides.

55. Liquid Amber *by Doreen Hooper, 1993. Fabric collage with machine and hand embroidery.*

57. Love Stones by Julia Caprara, early 1970s.
Hand embroidery and natural forms. Photograph by
the '62 Group.

Now we shall look at two examples of the work of Julia Caprara. I have been fortunate to watch her embroideries grow, change and develop for a number of years. The constant factor is the sensitive way she approaches and handles her materials. *Love Stones* (Fig. 57) is part of a series of work on the theme of love and exploring the qualities of moss and lichen, which lovingly 'hug' surfaces in nature. The textile component is a number of embroidered stitches, such as eyelets, buttonhole and French knots on scrim, with canvas embroidery and crewel wools, in conjunction with other threads such as perlé, silks and coton à broder. It is amazing how the embroideries work so well with the natural flints to which they are attached, without looking at all contrived or awkward.

This kind of sensitive combination of seemingly disparate elements is an inspiration to us all; it shows that everything can be made to harmonize with everything else.

But when I see the dimples in her face
All filled with tender moss in every place—
Ah, then I think, when all is said and done,
My favourite flower must be a mossy stone!

W.H. Davies, *Flowers*

Sphagnum Pool (Fig. 58), also by Julia Caprara, is a glorious mass of organized tangles, knots and loops, dangling, languishing and drooping, all evocative of pond life. Here again we see an extraordinary range of materials and techniques used to create an image of mysterious secrecy and luscious completeness. Julia Caprara describes her work:

58. Sphagnum Pool by Julia Caprara, 1974. Hand embroidery and mixed media. Photograph by the '62 Group.

Sphagnum Pool is a hand-embroidered and mixed media wall-hung textile. Eyelets, French knots, fringing, buttonhole stitch, small woven pieces, wrapped threads and wires, knitted pieces. Padded, quilted and built up over a fibre-glass-moulded cascade section for a garden pool. Hand-embroidered on scrim using tapestry, crewel and knitting yarns, crochet cotton, stranded threads, silk wire, wooden and handmade papier maché beads. Moulded fibre-glass base. Developed as a relief sculptural form based on the concept of the deep mystery and secret places of rock pools and the mossy banks and overhung shadowed pools.

CONCLUSION OF THE PROJECT

The final stages of this project consist of three hand techniques. The first is to enrich the surface as a whole by covering it with tiny seed stitches. These can be made with any threads you like, but try to match tones and colours with the fabric so that the stitches enhance what is there already.

The second stage is to construct the web. Madeira Threads supply metallic threads which have a gossamer-like appearance; although intended for machine use, they can equally well be sewn by hand. I chose a mid-toned thread, multicoloured like mother-of-pearl. I constructed the web with hand stitching, couching each strand with another thread to keep them secure. See if you can find and use a thread like this because the way it catches the light as you sew is quite entrancing.

The third and final stage is to sew beads on to the web to represent dewdrops. It is important that these are not too obviously stated, lest they negate the delicacy of the web. Choose clear glass beads so that they show up only when the light catches them. It is also important that their small size should vary slightly; if they are all the same size, they may appear relentlessly uniform. In Fig. 54 you will notice only a few of these beads in spite of the fact that there are several hundred of them hanging on the web. As with dewdrops in real life, they are not all seen from one viewpoint. One of the attractive qualities of

embroidery is that it looks different from various viewpoints.

Although this project may have taken you quite a long time to complete, as it did me, I hope you have found pleasure in making it.

When a man faces his maker, he will have to account for those pleasures of life he failed to experience.

The Talmud

The Squirrel, The Fox and Harvest Mice

Animals are such agreeable friends – they ask no questions, they pass no criticisms.

George Eliot

To conclude our autumn chapter let us make three pictures concurrently, with some friends of the countryside as our subjects. We can use these projects to practise our expertise in all the creative skills we have been investigating. Our abilities in various techniques, creating colour harmonies, balance in design and composition always need nurturing and developing.

Many of us find the sight of a grey squirrel foraging for nuts amongst the crisp fallen leaves a frequent delight. Less frequent is the sight of a fox at rest or a harvest mouse displaying his acrobatic prowess on corn stems. We may need to look for such images in natural history books and magazines; maybe we know a friend who has taken photographs or an artist who has painted these animals. All such visual sources will help us with our designs. *The Squirrel* (Fig. 59) and *Harvest Mice* (Fig. 60) are derived from a

59. The Squirrel, *1992. Fabric collage with machine
and hand embroidery.*

number of images from some of my natural history books. *The Fox* (Fig. 61) is derived from just one source; it is my free interpretation of a watercolour painting by Archibald Thorburn, the early-twentieth-century naturalist illustrator and artist.

All three embroideries were constructed in the same way. To start with, all the collage pieces were cut very small. Those which formed the animals were placed in directions to equate with the lie of their fur. Those which formed the area around the animals were placed in corresponding and complementary directions, to create a rhythmic balance. At the first machine embroi-

dery stage, the zigzag stitches followed the same direction as did the straight stitches at the hand and second machine embroidery stages.

The purpose of the final machine embroidery stage, as no doubt you are becoming aware, is sometimes to subdue as well as enhance. We need to make assessments all the time; sometimes we need to adjust parts of our pictures which seem out of harmony with the rest, sometimes we need to enrich parts of our pictures.

As you make these projects, I hope you are constantly reassuring and encouraging yourselves in all your endeavours in our journey together through the seasons of the countryside.

61. The Fox, *1992. Fabric collage with machine and hand embroidery. The detail (right) shows the stitches and collage pieces placed in the same direction as the lie of the animal's fur.*

60. *Left:* Harvest Mice, *1992. Fabric collage with machine and hand embroidery.*

CHAPTER FOUR

Winter

Who knoweth if to die
be but to live…
And that called life
by mortals
be but death?

Euripides

Some people see winter as the death of the year, but it is also a resting period, a time to replenish spent energies and a season of preparation for new activity. We have learnt how important it is to rest between our activities. So also, it seems, it is important for the year to have a season of rest to prepare itself for the other three busy seasons.

We also shall treat this season restfully. We shall still work at our projects but, rather than exploring anything radically new in terms of method and technique, we shall behave in a more reflective and contemplative fashion. We shall revise those procedures, processes and techniques which we have attempted before. However, there will not be so much technical instruction and more emphasis will be given to the introduction of new subjects. These will present compositional challenges, particularly relating to the colour schemes which this season offers: sometimes stark, sometimes subtle, but always stimulating.

62. Christmas Morning, 1993. Fabric collage with machine and hand embroidery. Photograph by Brian Nevitt.

In this way, you will be able to use this last chapter to consolidate everything you have learnt. By applying your knowledge in different ways, with help and guidance, you will be preparing yourself to venture alone for the first time. Consider it, then, as the winter prelude to the spring of your future independent activity.

> *It is not death, but plenitude of peace;*
> *And the dim cloud that does the world enfold*
> *Hath less the characters of dark and cold*
> *Than warmth and light asleep,*
> *And corresponding breathing seems to keep*
> *With the infant harvest, breathing soft below*
> *Its eider coverlet of snow.*
> *Nor is in field or garden anything*
> *But, duly look'd into, contains serene*
> *The substance of things hoped for, in the Spring,*
> *And evidence of Summer not yet seen.*

Coventry Patmore, *Winter*

The Dormouse

THE INSPIRATION

The dormouse also likes a rest period. As a rule, he hibernates from October or November right through to March or April. Occasionally, he interrupts his winter sleep with a few days' activity, particularly if there is a spell of fine weather. Imagine, then, that we are experiencing a few mild days at the start of this, our 'Winter' chapter, and we have glimpsed the tawny coat and bushy tail of the little dormouse in some nearby hazel trees.

THE PROJECT FROM START TO FINISH

First remember to practise the 'Golden Cord' exercise (see page 6).

Fig. 63 shows my interpretation of this subject. It is a small detail of an embroidery whose dimensions are only 18 × 18mm (7 × 7in). This detail enables you to examine the technique closely. The method consists of fabric collage, machine and hand embroidery; the procedure is the same as we followed for our last three projects, *The Squirrel*, *The Fox*, and *Harvest Mice*.

Examine Fig. 63 again and you will notice that some metallic threads have been used. If you do use any fabric or thread which reflects the light, it is advisable to place it only in shadowed areas. Look at any metallic object, for example a ring or wristwatch casing, and you will see that as much of it is in darkness as in light, if not more so. Because of this, if you use reflective materials in areas of your picture which you wish to be constantly of a pale tone, you may be dismayed to find the dark aspects always presenting themselves! I have therefore deliberately sewn metallic threads only in the dark parts of this picture. It is inappropriate to have dark passages where a constantly pale tone is required, but it can be interesting to allow the occasional gleam of light to shine out of dark shadows.

Let us now look at the same subject in reverse. One of the most important elements in my picture are the highlights in the dormouse's eyes. In this case, it was essential that I used a matt cotton to ensure the constancy of the pale tone.

Thus, not only is it necessary to observe nature, we also need to be aware of the nature of the materials we are using in order to manifest our responses in the most appropriate way. You will remember how we discussed this in *The Blackberries and the Spider's Web in the Hedgerow* project (page 77).

> *There is no Art delivered to mankind that hath*
> *not the works of Nature for his principal object.*

Sir Philip Sidney

63. The Dormouse, *1993. Fabric collage with*
machine and hand embroidery.

TIME TO PAUSE FOR RESTFUL THOUGHT

Before we go on to our next project, let us look at Fig. 64, a picture of an owl. Margaret Flintham started it on one of my courses and completed it at home. The method and technique is the same as for the dormouse and for the preceding three projects, but with a few variations. One of these is the hand stitching for the eyes, which creates a startling effect. The way the fabric has been cut and positioned is also very important because the outward-moving direction imparts a dynamic, almost explosive, quality. It almost seems as if we can hear the owl hooting his melancholy cry! Margaret has used a large variety of different browns and the repetition of similar colours has a unifying effect,

whereas the sudden changes and contrasts of tone give liveliness and vivacity to the picture. It is a fine example of how line, colour and tone are used not only for descriptive, but also for dramatic, purpose.

The Robin

THE INSPIRATION

Most birds fly away when you approach, but the robin often comes close when you are digging in the garden, even sitting on top of your spade. Apparently this friendliness is a unique characteristic of our native species; those on the

64. The Owl *by Margaret Flintham, 1993. Fabric collage with machine and hand embroidery.*

Continent are shy, retiring birds. The sweetness of his song is cheering even on the most dreary winter days. He is also admired for his bright red breast. All these characteristics make the robin one of the best loved of all our wild birds. Let us now make a picture of him perched on a branch of a holly tree.

The redbreast warbles still, but is content
With slender notes, and more than half
  suppressed:
Pleased with his solitude, and flitting light
From spray to spray, where'er he rests he shakes
From many a twig the pendant drops of ice,
That twinkle in the withered leaves below.

William Cowper, *The Task*

THE PROJECT FROM START TO FINISH

If you look at Fig. 65 you will see that we shall again be engaged in the 'drawing with the needle' technique, which we tried for the first time in *The Silver Birches* project. My pictures of *Sunrise* and *Sunset* (Figs. 1 and 74) are also executed by means of this technique, but carried out in different ways. So why not explore a different way yourself?

Fig. 65 is an exercise in harmonizing the complementary colours red and green. First the main contours of the composition, including the outline of the green leaves, were drawn with a red thread. This established a continuity right from the start. In turn, the many variations of green, some pale blues and mid- to dark-toned browns

65. The Robin, *1993. Free machine embroidery.*

were taken through the composition. A number of variegated threads were also used, including a particularly interesting Madeira thread composed of very pale blue, green and extremely pale red ('pink').

The many variations of one stitch help to develop the composition in a constructive manner. By 'constructive', I mean that the stitch directions should follow the contours of the forms within the picture, rather than 'filling in' the outlines any old way!

TIME TO PAUSE FOR RESTFUL THOUGHT

From hidden bulb the flower reared up
Its angled, slender, cold, dark stem,
Whence dangled an inverted cup
  For tri-leaved diadem.
Beneath these ice-pure sepals lay
A triplet of green-pencilled snow,
Which in the chill-aired gloom of day
  Stirred softly to and fro.

Walter De La Mare, *The Snowdrop*

Before we become involved in the final projects for this season and, indeed, of our journey together through the countryside, I should like to look at some snowdrops which have been embroidered especially for this book by Maureen King (see Figs. 66 and 67). Maureen loves to work on a very small scale and enjoys hand stitching enormously. In the original sense of the word, she is a true amateur because she does it for love.

There is an obvious pleasure in Maureen's execution of her purse, matching pincushion and scissors' case. The snowdrops are embroidered on pink silk noil. The stalks are constructed with stem stitch, using just one thread of stranded cotton in a single green colour. This single colour acts as a foil to the space-dyed thread used for the leaves, which are worked in broad chain stitch. The centres of the snowdrops are created by partly covering freshwater pearls with detached buttonhole stitch. The petals are made by a method of needle-weaving which

forms picots; the picots are partly free-standing and so bring the embroidery into relief. Thus we behold an innovative form of stumpwork, which was immensely popular in Elizabethan and Jacobean times.

From its inception to its final stitch, this whole project is infused with a delicate and exquisite beauty which makes me wonder whether Maureen saw 'heaven' in the snowdrops which inspired her.

To see a world in a grain of sand
And heaven in a wild flower.
Behold infinity in the palm of your hand
And eternity in an hour.

William Blake

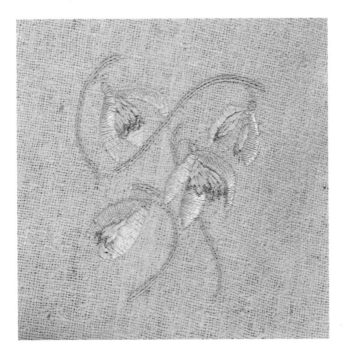

66. Snowdrops *purse, pincushion and scissors case by Maureen King, 1993. Hand-embroidered stumpwork, stranded cotton on silk noil.*
(Above) 67. Detail.

The Snow Scene

Old January clad in crispy rime,
Comes hirpling on and often makes a stand;
The hasty snowstorm ne'er disturbs his time
He mends no pace but beats his dithering hand.

John Clare

THE INSPIRATION

One of the wonders nature has in store for us is when snow spreads its white winter coat over the landscape. I always thrill to its strange enchantment.

THE PROJECT FROM START TO FINISH

Let us try to emulate the paradox of the richness of such a chilling winter sight. Fig. 68 shows a snow scene composed entirely in black and white. It seemed appropriate to use this limitation to convey the severities and harshness of snow. However, in order to portray its splendid

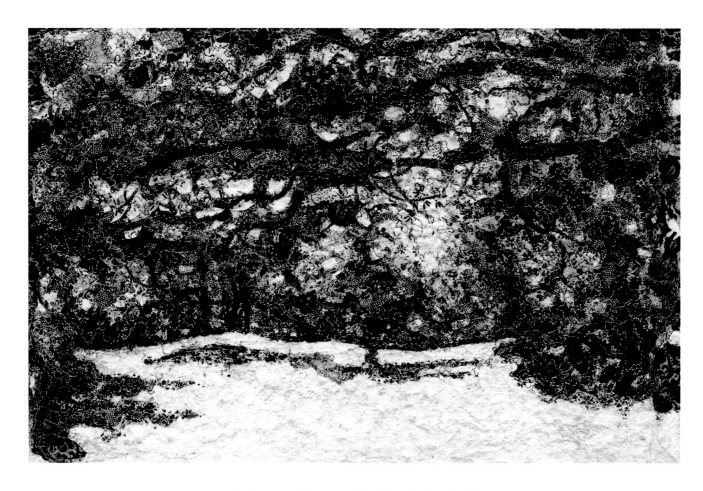

68. The Snow Scene, *mid-1980s. Black-and-white
fabric collage with machine and hand embroidery.*

and sumptuous qualities, I chose as many different kinds of fabrics and threads as possible so
that the surface of the embroidery was rich in
texture. Start as always be practising the 'Golden
Cord' exercise (see page 6) so that you become
restfully attentive, then seek out all your white
and black pieces of fabric from your ragbag. You
may be surprised, as I was, to find how many
'colours' you will see within this apparent limitation. You will probably notice that some of
your whites are ever so slightly yellow and take
on the appearance of cream, whereas others are
tinged with blue, red or, indeed, any of the
colours of the spectrum. Likewise, you may find
that your blacks are also very slightly coloured
in this way.

Try also to find transparent fabrics such as
organdie, lace, gauze and net. You will discover
that, as you layer these substances over each
other, from a distance they will give the illusion
of grey. According to the density of each type of
material and how many layers you use, you will
find that you can modulate the tonal values
from light to dark quite considerably. I have to
admit that I found this out quite by accident,
and as a result discarded all the grey fabric I had
originally intended to use! The illusion of grey
by this means was a far more exciting challenge.

The method of the picture's construction was
our now-familiar combination of fabric collage,
machine and hand embroidery. The final stage
was to embellish the surface with a random mixture of beads and sequins, whose common factor
is that they are either black or white. See how

69. Winter *by Eirian Short, 1991. Hand embroidery.*
Photograph by Eirian Short.

you manage this project. I believe you will find the limitation an interesting and challenging discipline to follow.

Instruction improves the innate powers, and good discipline strengthens the heart.

Horace

TIME TO PAUSE FOR RESTFUL THOUGHT

Let us look at some other depictions of winter for inspiration on the many different variations of landscape which this season offers us.

Fig. 69 illustrates a winter scene by Eirian Short when the snow is beginning to melt and reveal new shoots pushing their way up through the leaves and bracken. Eirian's stitch directions are always an important factor in her work, giving interest and vitality to her compositions. Here you will perceive a number of complementary opposites: verticals complementing horizontals, and opposing curves and angles resolving each other. There is also the strong contrast of light and dark, and the less obvious but nonetheless crucial resolution of the subtle brownish-orange of the leaves with the greyish-blue of the sky. These opposites and complementaries are brought together to form a harmonious equilibrium.

Old Year Leaves

The leaves which in the autumn of the year
Fall auburn-tinted, leaving reft and bare
Their parent trees, in many a sheltered lair
Where winter waits and watches, cold, austere,
Will lie in drifts; and when the snowdrop cheer
The woodland shadows, still the leaves are there,
Though through the glades the balmy southern air
And birds on boughs proclaim that Spring is here.

Mackenzie Bell

Let us now look at a lovely scene which is gentle, lyrical, almost romantic. Fig. 70 shows Pauline Thomas's embroidery *Hedgethorn*. Her method is to paint the silk backing fabric first with fabric dyes, and then to machine embroider her composition with matching and contrasting threads. I particularly wanted to include Pauline's work in this book because of her ability to combine a number of different and seemingly disparate techniques. Many of us would find it difficult to resolve both dyes and stitches. Often one medium, usually the dye, is dominated by the other. This is not the case here; both have equal value and each enhances and augments the other. Notice also how the subtle blue hues of the trees and clouds are complemented by very pale orange-red tints in the sky and reflected lights on the snow-covered field. Pauline Thomas's own description of her work suggests its lyrical beauty:

Nature's summer clothing now gone, reveals the ivy silhouettes on the winter trees. The pruny berries remain from autumn feasting. The raucous sound of gathering crows echoes around the cool halls of an English winter.

After the gentle lyricism of the last scene, the detail in Margaret Hall-Townley's *Thorn Tree* (Fig. 71) is a marked contrast. It conjures up all the severest aspects of the winter season: harsh, cruel and relentless qualities are all portrayed in this truly dramatic and wonderful embroidery. The spiky thorns, the angry twists and contorted angles in the trunk and branches are tenderly delineated by straight machine stitching. Once again, the multifarious stitch directions are resolved. Although the *depiction* is harsh and severe, there is nothing harsh or severe in its *execution*. All the various elements of line, tone and colour come together in perfect equilibrium. There is a new quality about this embroidery which we have not met before — its surface is convoluted. This is achieved by embroidering the fabric without a frame. As the machine stitching becomes more and more dense, the fabric is manipulated to form these interesting undulations which catch the light and cast

70. Hedgethorn by Pauline Thomas, 1993. Machine embroidery on hand-painted silk. Photograph by Pauline Thomas.

71. Thorn Tree *by Margaret Hall-Townley, 1993.*
Free machine embroidery.

open, uncrowded design has an atmosphere of silence and solitude, on which we might like to muse and meditate.

> *Happy the man, whose wish and care*
> *A few paternal acres bound,*
> *Content to breathe his native air,*
>   *In his own ground.*
> *Whose herds with milk, whose fields with bread,*
> *Whose flocks supply him with attire;*
> *Whose trees in summer yield him shade,*
>   *In winter fire.*

Alexander Pope, *Solitude*

Christmas Morning

THE INSPIRATION

And now we come to our last major project. An oil painting (Fig. 73) acts as our guide for the embroidery which opened this chapter (Fig. 62).

The painting took two winters to do many years ago. I began it during the Christmas holidays when I was teaching full-time. Somehow or other I did not bring the composition to a satisfactory conclusion. When I was packing to go to the same place the following Christmas I suddenly remembered the picture and took it with me to see if I could complete it. For days I fiddled around with it but made little progress until Christmas morning revealed a thick frost across the entire landscape. Attired in layers of woolly jumpers, several pairs of socks and mittens, I spent a splendid couple of hours as this thrilling sight seemed to suggest effortlessly how the painting should be resolved. Many artists described how such things occur in spite of themselves, and now it had happened to me. It was a splendid Christmas present!

strange and curious shadows. The resulting three-dimensional effect contributes to the dramatic intensity of the scene.

In Fig. 72 you will find a winter landscape which manifests yet another character. Miranda Brookes portrays a scene which is milder and more temperate; indeed, we can see the mist rising off the ground. Compared to the clarity of Margaret Hall-Townley's contours, all the forms in Miranda's embroidery are suggested. She has diffused all her main contours so that their edges are implied. Not only does this create a misty effect, it also invites us to use our imagination in order to complete the outlines and contours. This and the horizontal aspect of the composition create a feeling of peace and stillness. The

72. Winter Landscape *by Miranda Brookes, early*
1990s. Mixed embroidery techniques. Photograph by
Miranda Brookes.

THE PROJECT FROM START TO FINISH

The method is our well-practised fabric collage combined with machine and hand embroidery. However, although this method is 'well-practised' by us, it is by no means fully realized. The new element upon which we are going to focus our attention is the colour. Although not as limited as our last project, *The Snow Scene*, it is very subdued but within its subtle range there is an interestingly large scope.

What swords and spears, what daggers bright
He arms the morning with! How light
His power is, that's fit to lie
On the wings of a butterfly!
What milk-white clothing he has made
For every little twig and blade!
What curious silver work is shown
On wood and iron, glass and stone!

W.H. Davies, *Frost*

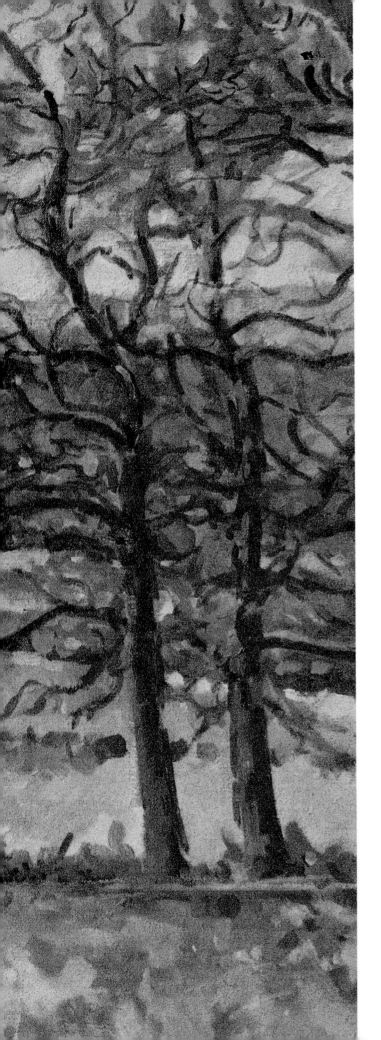

First seek out all the grey fabrics in your rag-bag and put them into various piles, determined by which colour of the spectrum they seem to be biased towards. Then do the same with your brown and white pieces of fabric. I think you will be surprised by the range of colour in this seemingly dull and limited group. The next thing is to find the palest blues, greens and pale red fabrics to mix with the whites for the sky and frosted areas of the landscape; then the most dull and mid-toned greens and blues to mix with the same-toned greys and browns for the trees and bushes.

Use the collage method (see page 17) in any way you like. You can cut up the fabric into tiny scraps and assemble them like a mosaic, or you may prefer to cut them more to shape. I used both these methods at this stage.

When you are ready to machine stitch the picture, select coloured threads to match the fabrics and choose any method you like to apply your fabric pieces to the backing material. I employed the widest zigzag stitch for the whole of this process, but varied its width to match the various sizes of fabric scraps over which I was travelling.

At the hand embroidery stage, select threads and yarns within the same colour and tonal range but do not be afraid to be daring. Raffia, garden twine and parcel string can harmonize happily with embroidery silks, weaving yarns and knitting wools!

If you wish to anchor your hand stitches with a further layer of machine embroidery, by all means do so. You may even like to embellish the entire surface with beads. Whatever you decide to do, remember to match and contrast your colours and tones appropriately so that as well as creating the illusion of a frosty landscape on Christmas morning, you are also creating a harmonious design in which all parts interrelate to form an integrated whole.

73. Christmas Morning, *1980-81. Oil painting.*

Sunset

The sun descending in the west,
The evening star does shine;
The birds are silent in their nest,
And I must seek for mine.
The moon like a flower
In heaven's high bower,
With silent delight
Sits and smiles on the night.

William Blake, *Night*

John Milton's 'bright morning star' illuminated the first steps of our journey together in the countryside through the seasons of the year. Now, as the sun descends on our journey, William Blake's 'evening star' shines on our final steps. So let us bring our creative spirit home to rest. As the Gaelic proverb says, 'Night is a good herdsman: she brings all creatures home.' Tomorrow you will venture boldly alone, for the first time, in search of truth and beauty in all your future projects.

'Beauty is truth, truth beauty', — that is all
Ye know on earth, and all ye need to know.

John Keats, *Ode On A Grecian Urn*

74. Sunset, 1993. Free machine embroidery.

Glossary

Analogy. A similarity, equivalent, metaphor, parable, simile, e.g. analogous colours are similar colours.

Analytical. Refers to the ability to abstract particular parts or specific relations from generalities.

Appliqué. The application of one material to another by means of stitching.

Assessment. The ability to observe objectively, and to understand what has been done and is being done.

Attention. The ability to be fully observant without being distracted by irrelevances.

Balance. Matching, bringing into equilibrium, regulating extreme differences, equalization.

Collage. The application of one material to another by means of sticking with an adhesive.

Colours. The constituent parts of decomposed rays of light and the general name given to those elements: red, orange, yellow, green, blue and violet.

Complementary. Refers to an element or quality which usually contrasts with, or is in opposition to, another element or quality.

Composition. The harmonious relation of all parts, elements and qualities of a whole.

Concurrent. The running or existing together of two or more activities to which attention is given alternatively but not simultaneously.

Configuration. The resulting shape, aspect or character produced by the relative position of its parts.

Contrast. The emphasis of differences between things, elements or qualities by close juxtaposition.

Couching. A form of stitching where one or more threads are attached to material by another thread.

Detail of The Honeysuckle and the Sweet-briar Rose *(see page 52).*

Cross hatching. A method of drawing by means of crossed parallel lines in order to achieve a type of shading or certain coloured effects.

Design. The plan or organization of all parts of an activity or embroidery, or any created object, to compose a coherent order and unity.

Drawing. The representation, portrayal and realization of a person's response to the world.

Elements. The components which contribute to the structure and substance of any created object such as edge, line, shape, form, tone, colour and texture.

Evaluation. The ability to recognize the value in that which has been done and is being done for present and future use.

Form. A shape which is often comprehended in three dimensions, but also sometimes understood in two dimensions.

Form (to). To create, construct and make.

Glazing. A term from oil painting. The transparent layering of thin films of pigment, used to achieve subtle and glossy coloured effects.

Granite stitch. Very dense machine stitching formed by close, straight stitches in small, overlapping circles.

Harmony. The balanced combination of constituent parts, elements and qualities to form a connected whole, usually comprising those that are both similar and complementary.

Hue. The quality that distinguishes one particular kind of colour from another, e.g. a blue-green and a yellow-green.

Inspiration. The influence infusing the thought, feeling and spirit ('breath') of the maker, thus animating the object created.

Integrity. The state of wholeness and completeness, entire in and of itself.

Intuition. The instinctive ability to make leaps of insight and creativity without analytical, logical and rational reasoning.

Knowledge. That which is discovered and understood (an empirical definition only).

Line. An edge or contour in either a straight or curved direction.

Local colour. The intrinsic colour of any particular object, e.g. a *yellow* buttercup.

Local colour tone. The intrinsic tonal value of any particular object, e.g. a *pale* green leaf.

Perception. The detection, recognition and understanding of sensations received from stimuli within the environment.

Procedure. The particular way of conducting, organizing and moving through a process or activity.

Process. An activity or course of actions.

Rational. Refers to the ability to make decisions based on information, facts and reasons.

Realization. That which has been portrayed, made manifest and real, e.g. a design or embroidery.

Rules. Guidelines to assist the procedure through a process, activity or course of actions.

Seed stitch. A very small straight stitch which can be made at any angle.

Sensitivity. The ability to be aware and appreciative of impressions in an objective manner.

Shade. A dark tone.

Shape. An area perceived in two dimensions.

Spacial. Refers to the ability to understand how individual parts relate to each other.

Straight stitching. (By hand) single stitches of any desired length or angle. (By machine) a continuous line consisting of single stitches, in any direction.

Stumpwork. Embroidery stitches and devices raised in relief from a ground fabric.

Tent stitch. A diagonal canvaswork stitch.

Texture. The surface quality of any physical substance.

Tint. A light or pale tone.

Tone. The quality that refers to any value within the range between light and dark.

Bibliography

Angus, Anne, *Hedgerow*, Partridge Press, 1987

Arnason, H.H., *A History of Modern Art*, Thames and Hudson, revised edition, 1977

Ashby, Eric, *The Secret Life of the New Forest*, Chatto & Windus, 1989

Benham, W. Gurney, *Cassell's Classified Quotations*, Cassell, 1921

Beningfield, Gordon, *Green and Pleasant Land*, Viking, 1989

Poems of the Countryside, Viking, 1987

Poems of the Seasons, Viking, 1992

Berrill, Frances and Exley, Helen, *A Gift of Flowers*, Exley Publishers, 1983

Bishop, Iain, *Thorburn's Mammals*, Book Club Associates, 1974

Bloomer, Carolyn M., *Principles of Visual Perception*, Van Nostrand Reinhold, 1976

Bonham-Carter, Victor, *A Posy of Wildflowers*, Allan Wingate, 1946

Clucas, Phillip, *Country Seasons*, Windward, 1978

Cotterell, Lawrence (ed.) *100 Favourite Poems of the Countryside*, Piatkus, 1990

Edwards, Betty, *Drawing on the Right Side of the Brain*, Souvenir Press, 1981

Edward, B.L. (ed.) *I am Gone into the Fields — An Anthology*, Ernest Benn, 1929

Felix Jiři, *Woodland and Hill Birds*, Octopus, 1983

Frank, Frederick, *The Zen of Seeing*, Alfred A. Knopf, Vintage Books edn, 1973

Gibran, Kahil, *The Prophet*, reprinted Heinemann, 1979

Grimes, Brian, *British Wild Animals*, Treasure Press, 1974

Hamilton, George Heard, *Painting and Sculpture in Europe 1880-1940*, Penguin, revised edition, 1978

Hanbury, Ada *Flower Painting*, Blackie & Son, 1885

Holden, Edith, *The Country Diary of an Edwardian Lady*, Webb and Bower, 1977

The Nature Notes of an Edwardian Lady, Webb and Bower, 1989

Jekyll, Gertrude, *Wood and Garden*, The Ayer Company, 1983

Kerr, Jessica, *Shakespeare's Flowers*, Longman, 1969

Klickman, Flora, *Flower Pictures by Maud Angell*, early 1900s

Tramping with a Colour Box by C.J. Vine, early 1900s

Leach, Michael, *The Secret Life of Snowdonia*, Chatto & Windus, 1991

Lowenfeld, Victor, *Creative and Mental Growth*, Macmillan, fifth edition, 1970

Malins, Frederick, *Understanding Paintings: The Elements of Composition*, Phaidon, 1980

Mantegazza, Paolo, *The Legends of Flowers*, T. Werner Laurie, 1930

McKim, Robert H., *Experiences in Visual Thinking*, Wadsworth, second edition, 1980

Murray, Peter and Linda, *A Dictionary of Arts and Artists*, Penguin, third edition, 1975

Mussen, Paul, H., Conger, John J. and Kagan, Jerome, *Child Development and Personality*, Harper & Row, fifth edition, 1979

Pickles, Sheila, *The Language of Flowers*, Pavilion, 1990

Richter, Irma A., *The Notebooks of Leonardo Da Vinci*, Oxford University Press, 1980

Searle, Lindley, *The Song of Flowers*, Staples Press, 1949

Shree Purohit Swami, *The Ten Principal Upanishads*, Faber and Faber, 1970

Smith, Guy N., *Animals of the Countryside*, Saiga Publishing, 1980

Swami Vivekananda, *Work and its Secret*, J.N. Dey at Union Press, seventh impression, 1976

Thomas, Mary, *Dictionary of Embroidery Stitches*, Hodder & Stoughton, 1934

Thomas, R.S. (ed.), *The Batsford Book of Country Verse*, B.T. Batsford, 1961

Wood, James, *The Nuttall Dictionary of Quotations*, Frederick Warne, 1930

Index

Page numbers in *italics* refer to illustrations